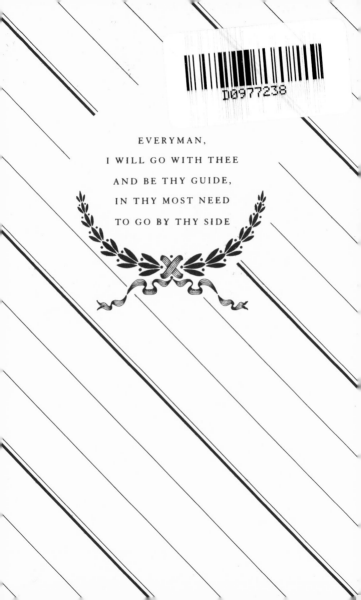

EVERYMAN,
I WILL GO WITH THEE
AND BE THY GUIDE,
IN THY MOST NEED
TO GO BY THY SIDE

EVERYMAN'S LIBRARY
POCKET POETS

On Wings of Song

Poems About Birds

Selected and edited by
J. D. McClatchy

EVERYMAN'S LIBRARY

POCKET POETS

Alfred A. Knopf · New York · Toronto

THIS IS A BORZOI BOOK
PUBLISHED BY ALFRED A. KNOPF

This selection by J. D. McClatchy first published in Everyman's Library,
2000
Copyright © 2000 by Everyman Publishers plc

Fourth printing

www.randomhouse.com/everymans

ISBN 0-375-40749-9

Typography by Peter B. Willberg
Typeset in the UK by AccComputing, North Barrow, Somerset
Printed and bound in Germany by GGP Media, Pössneck

CONTENTS

NESTS AND CAGES

BIRDSONG

FLIGHTS OF FANCY

FOREWORD

At the very dawn of civilization, birds were symbols of the spirit. Falcon or dove, stork or raven or owl, they were our messengers, fierce or gentle intermediaries between our earthbound lives and the upper air. In Egyptian hieroglyphs, Greek myths, Biblical accounts, tribal chants, and popular legend, they were omens and emblems to be longed for or feared. Always and everywhere, with their uncanny freedom and their exquisite song, they were our sense of soul, the premonition and instance of a life beyond our own.

Scientists now tell us birds are descended from dinosaurs, miniature versions of gigantic powers. We can feel them in our backs: we can flex our fleshed-over wings, yet feel the weight of our bodies below; we can sing earnestly in the shower, and be shamed by the effortless trill out the window. Above all, we envy the power of flight, the way it annihilates distance and assures safety. We long for their lonely, soaring elegance, and some of our most remarkable heroes – from Icarus to Lindbergh to the weightless space-walker – have intrigued the human imagination by their resemblance to birds, our gliding, looping, hovering skyriders.

"Sir," remarked Samuel Johnson, "we are a nest of singing birds." Down the centuries, poets especially have been drawn to birds as the embodiment of their vocation at its most transcendent: to ascend, like Shakespeare's lark, to heaven's gate. "The bird," wrote the French poet St.-John Perse, "is he who bears hidden in himself, to nourish his passions, the highest fever of the blood. His grace is that burning." A bird's deliberate, passionate performance – carried out, as Matthew Arnold once observed, "beside us, but alone" – is the shadow cast overhead by a poet's own flights of fancy.

Even a book open in the hand will look like a bird. In this one a reader will find first what is most familiar, those birds we see and hear most often near the nests – house or barn – we have built for ourselves. To a poet's eye, even the most domesticated bird keeps an eerie strangeness about itself, like the shrill felicity of Emily Dickinson's bluejay. We next branch out to discover more elusive birds in their natural habitats: forest, field, pond, empyrean. In so many of these poems, creature and element are one, a single entity we are drawn to and kept from. Everything in nature has a side that repels or frightens or amuses us, and so the vulture or ostrich are given their turns. Certain other birds – nightingale, peacock, swan – have acquired a unique symbolic status. They have come in countless re-tellings to represent particular human traits, from wisdom to vanity, and the history of poetry abounds with exquisite little allegories. We then pass on to other sorts of habitats, the nest and the cage. In this anthology's final sections, whose poets range from Virgil to Chaucer, from Wordsworth to Yeats, from Poe to Frost, small birds give rise to meditations on grand themes. It's not what birds are or do, but what they remind us of about ourselves, that is the focus. And brought together here are some of the most inspired and beloved poems ever written. Whether it's the hijinks of "The Owl and the Pussy-Cat" or the sweet sadness of "Ode to a Nightingale," here is poetry's best tribute to our very human longings for wonder and escape, and to the airborne imagination that sings of what is past, or passing, or to come.

J. D. McCLATCHY

THE
BACKYARD

SHORT CIRCUIT

For no reason,
all at once,

a dove and a jay
swerve and land

at opposite ends
of the clothesline,

and the clothes – mine,
all mine! – commence

to dance with reckless
love and joy.

THE JAY

No Brigadier throughout the Year
So civic as the Jay –
A Neighbor and a Warrior too
With shrill felicity
Pursuing Winds that censure us
A February Day,
The Brother of the Universe
Was never blown away –
The Snow and he are intimate –
I've often seen them play
When Heaven looked upon us all
With such severity
I felt apology were due
To an insulted sky
Whose pompous frown was Nutriment
To their Temerity –
The Pillow of this daring Head
Is pungent Evergreens –
His Larder – terse and Militant –
Unknown – refreshing things –
His Character – a Tonic –
His Future – a Dispute –
Unfair an Immortality
That leaves this Neighbor out –

JENNY WREN

Of all the birds that rove and sing,
　　　Near dwellings made for men,
None is so nimble, feat, and trim,
　　　　As Jenny Wren.

With pin-point bill, and tail a-cock,
　　　So wildly shrill she cries,
The echoes on his roof-tree knock
　　　　And fill the skies.

Never was sweeter seraph hid
　　　Within so small a house –
A tiny, inch-long, eager, ardent,
　　　　Feathered mouse.

NUTHATCH

Quick, at the feeder, pausing
Upside down, in its beak
A sunflower seed held tight
To glance by chestnut, dust-blue,
White, an eye-streak
Gone in a blurred ripple
Straight to the cedar branch
To the trunk to a crevice
In bark and putting it
In there, quick, with the others,
Then arrowing straight back
For just one more all morning.

THE MOCKINGBIRD

Look one way and the sun is going down,
Look the other and the moon is rising.
The sparrow's shadow's longer than the lawn.
The bats squeak: "Night is here"; the birds cheep:
    "Day is gone."
On the willow's highest branch, monopolizing
Day and night, cheeping, squeaking, soaring,
The mockingbird is imitating life.

All day the mockingbird has owned the yard.
As light first woke the world, the sparrows trooped
Onto the seedy lawn: the mockingbird
Chased them off shrieking. Hour by hour, fighting hard
To make the world his own, he swooped
On thrushes, thrashers, jays, and chickadees –
At noon he drove away a big black cat.

Now, in the moonlight, he sits here and sings.
A thrush is singing, then a thrasher, then a jay –
Then, all at once, a cat begins meowing.
A mockingbird can sound like anything.
He imitates the world he drove away
So well that for a minute, in the moonlight,
Which one's the mockingbird? which one's the world?

RANDALL JARRELL   23

MOCKINGBIRD MONTH

A pupa of pain, I sat and lay one July,
companioned by the bird the Indians called "four
    hundred
tongues." Through the dark in the back yard by my bed,
through the long day near my front couch, the bird
sang without pause an amplified song "two-thirds
his own," books told me, "and one-third mimicry."

Gray charmer, "the lark and nightingale in one,"
unremitting maker of music so full of wit
and improvisation, I strained by night and light
to hear the scientists' record: "In ten minutes
he mimicked thirty-two species." I counted eight
(even I) variations on cardinal's song alone.

Cock of the neighborhood, his white flashes of wing
and long distinguished tail ruled the bushes and
    boughs,
and once, enchanted, I saw him walk past my house,
herding, from three feet behind, the neighbor's nice,
cowardly cat. He controlled without any fuss
but took little time off. Most of our month he sang.

The sticky wings of my mind began to open.
No mere plagiarist, a Harold Bloom singer,

he leaned on, but played with, robin or jay or
starling or whippoorwill. I began to prefer
him and house and hurting to the world outdoors.
Both art and art-lover attend to what may happen.

The weeks went by. At two A.M. he'd begin
my steadier, stronger, surer flight through his airs,
and the sun sent us into heights of his lyric together.
Virtuoso though he was, I was learning his repertoire.
Who would have thought the moth of me would tire?
Toward the end of a month in concert I began
     to complain.

Constant cadence, I told him, gives one no rest.
Is it my fault you must be lonesome for a mate?
There must be no nestlings to feed (when do *you* eat?).
What master of complexity won't duplicate
with incessant singing? Delete, delete, delete,
shut up for a while my bird-brained, brilliant stylist!

I left him for the North and less prolific birds
(but not before reading a chatty chapter on him
by a man who threw a shoe treeward at four A.M.
to stop "that endless torrent"), my movement
     a handsome
tribute to his voice. Leaving my pencils at home,
I resolved to husband my own apprentice words.

JUNCOS

They operate from elsewhere,
some hall in the mountains –
quick visit, gone.
Specialists on branch ends,
craft union. I like their
clean little coveralls.

THE ROBIN

My old Welsh neighbor over the way
    Crept slowly out in the sun of spring,
Pushed from her ears the locks of gray,
    And listened to hear the robins sing.

Her grandson, playing at marbles, stopped,
    And, cruel in sport as boys will be,
Tossed a stone at the bird, who hopped
    From bough to bough in the apple-tree.

"Nay!" said the grandmother; "have you not heard,
    My poor, bad boy! of the fiery pit,
And how, drop by drop, this merciful bird
    Carries the water that quenches it?

"He brings cool dew in his little bill,
    And lets it fall on the souls of sin:
You can see the mark on his red breast still
    Of fires that scorch as he drops it in.

"My poor Bron rhuddyn! my breast-burned bird,
    Singing so sweetly from limb to limb,
Very dear to the heart of Our Lord
    Is he who pities the lost like Him!"

"Amen!" I said to the beautiful myth;
    "Sing, bird of God, in my heart as well:
Each good thought is a drop wherewith
    To cool and lessen the fires of hell.

"Prayers of love like rain-drops fall,
    Tears of pity are cooling dew,
And dear to the heart of Our Lord are all
    Who suffer like Him in the good they do!"

THE STARLING

The starling is my darling, although
I don't much approve of its
Habits. Proletarian bird,
Nesting in holes and corners, making a mess,
And sometimes dropping its eggs
Just any old where – on the front lawn, for instance.

It thinks it can sing too. In springtime
They are on every rooftop, or high bough,
Or telegraph pole, blithering away
Discords, with clichés picked up
From the other melodists.

But go to Trafalgar Square,
And stand, about sundown, on the steps of
      St. Martin's;
Mark then, in the air,
The starlings, before they roost, at their evolutions –
Scores of starlings, wheeling,
Streaming and twisting, the whole murmuration
Turning like one bird: an image
Realized, of the City.

TO A SPARROW

Your perch is the branch
and your boudoir the branch also.
The branch, the rough branch!
evergreen boughs closing you about
like ironed curtains
to complete the decor.

The sun pours in
as the roughing wind blows
and who will conceive the luxury,
the rare lightness of
your fluttering toilette like him,
he who is lost and alone in the world?

Princess of the airy kingdoms
the sky is your wardrobe
and yellow roses
the frilled chrysanthemums bending
to the late season your park.

Among the clouds your couriers
post to embassies
beyond our fondest dreams
and heaven, the ancient court of saints
whispers to us
among the hemlocks
insistently of you.

HOUSE SPARROWS
for Joe and U. T. Summers

Not of the wealthy, Coral Gables class
Of travelers, nor that rarified tax bracket,
These birds weathered the brutal, wind-chill facts
Under our eaves, nesting in withered grass,
Wormless but hopeful, and now their voice enacts
Forsythian spring with primavernal racket.

Their color is the elderly, moleskin gray
Of doggedness, of mist, magnolia bark.
Salt of the earth, they are; the common clay;
Meek *émigrés* come over on the Ark
In steerage from the Old Country of the Drowned
To settle down along Long Island Sound,

Flatbush, Weehawken, our brownstone tenements,
Wherever the local idiom is *Cheep.*
Savers of string, meticulous and mild,
They are given to nervous flight, the troubled sleep
Of those who remember terrible events,
The wide-eyed, anxious haste of the exiled.

Like all the poor, their safety lies in numbers
And hardihood and anonymity
In a world of dripping browns and duns and umbers.

31

They have inherited the lower sky,
Their Lake of Constants, their blue modality
That they are borne upon and battered by.

Those little shin-bones, hollow at the core,
Emaciate finger-joints, those fleshless wrists,
Wrapped in a wrinkled, loose, rice-paper skin,
As though the harvests of earth had never been,
Where have we seen such frailty before?
In pictures of Biafra and Auschwitz.

Yet here they are, these chipper stratoliners,
Unsullen, unresentful, full of the grace
Of cheerfulness, who seem to greet all comers
With the wild confidence of Forty-Niners,
And, to the lively honor of their race,
Rude canticles of "Summers, Summers, Summers."

PIGEONS

The pigeons swing across the square,
Suddenly voiceless in midair,
Flaunting, against their civic coats,
The glossy oils that scarf their throats.

PIGEONS ON THE GRASS

Pigeons on the grass alas.
Pigeons on the grass alas.
Short longer grass short longer longer shorter
yellow grass Pigeons large pigeons on the shorter
longer yellow grass alas pigeons on the grass.
If they were not pigeons what were they.
If they were not pigeons on the grass alas what
were they. He had heard of a third and he asked about it
it was a magpie in the sky. If a magpie in the sky on the
sky can not cry if the pigeon on the grass alas can alas
and to pass the pigeon on the grass alas and the magpie
in the sky on the sky and to try and to try alas on the
grass alas the pigeon on the grass the pigeon on the
grass and alas. They might be very well very well very
well they might be they might be very well they might
be very well very well they might be.

THE
BARNYARD

TURKEYS

The turkeys wade the close to catch the bees
In the old border full of maple trees
And often lay away and breed and come
And bring a brood of chelping chickens home.
The turkey gobbles loud and drops his rag
And struts and sprunts his tail and then lets drag
His wing on ground and makes a huzzing noise,
Nauntles at passer-bye and drives the boys
And bounces up and flies at passer-bye.
The old dog snaps and grins nor ventures nigh.
He gobbles loud and drives the boys from play;
They throw their sticks and kick and run away.

JOHN CLARE   37

A BLACK NOVEMBER TURKEY
to A.M. and A.M.

Nine white chickens come
With haunchy walk and heads
Jabbing among the chips, the chaff, the stones
And the cornhusk-shreds,

And bit by bit infringe
A pond of dusty light,
Spectral in shadow until they bobbingly one
By one ignite.

Neither pale nor bright,
The turkey-cock parades
Through radiant squalors, darkly auspicious as
The ace of spades,

Himself his own cortège
And puffed with the pomp of death,
Rehearsing over and over with strangled râle
His latest breath.

The vast black body floats
Above the crossing knees
As a cloud over thrashed branches, a calm ship
Over choppy seas,

Shuddering its fan and feathers
In fine soft clashes
With the cold sound that the wind makes, fondling
    Paper-ashes.

The pale-blue bony head
Set on its shepherd's-crook
Like a saint's death-mask, turns a vague, superb
    And timeless look

Upon these clocking hens
And the cocks that one by one,
Dawn after mortal dawn, with vulgar joy
    Acclaim the sun.

RICHARD WILBUR   39

TURKEYS OBSERVED

One observes them, one expects them;
Blue-breasted in their indifferent mortuary,
Beached bare on the cold marble slabs
In immodest underwear frills of feather.

The red sides of beef retain
Some of the smelly majesty of living:
A half-cow slung from a hook maintains
That blood and flesh are not ignored.

But a turkey cowers in death.
Pull his neck, pluck him, and look –
He is just another poor forked thing,
A skin bag plumped with inky putty.

He once complained extravagantly
In an overture of gobbles;
He lorded it on the claw-flecked mud
With a grey flick of his Confucian eye.

Now, as I pass the bleak Christmas dazzle,
I find him ranged with his cold squadrons:
The fuselage is bare, the proud wings snapped,
The tail-fan stripped down to a shameful rudder.

CHAUNTECLEER
from "The Nun's Priest's Tale"

A yeerd she hadde, enclosed al aboute
With stikkes, and a drye dych withoute,
In which she hadde a cok, hight Chauntecleer.
In al the land, of crowyng nas his peer.
His voys was murier than the murie orgon
On messe-dayes that in the chirche gon.
Wel sikerer was his crowyng in his logge
Than is a clokke or an abbey orlogge.
By nature he knew ech ascencioun
Of the equynoxial in thilke toun;
For whan degrees fiftene weren ascended,
Thanne crew he, that it myghte nat been amended.
His coomb was redder than the fyn coral,
And batailled as it were a castel wal;
His byle was blak, and as the jeet it shoon;
Lyk asure were his legges and his toon;
His nayles whitter than the lylye flour,
And lyk the burned gold was his colour.
This gentil cok hadde in his governaunce
Sevene hennes for to doon al his plesaunce,
Whiche were his sustres and his paramours,
And wonder lyk to hym, as of colours;
Of whiche the faireste hewed on hir throte
Was cleped faire damoysele Pertelote.

Curteys she was, discreet, and debonaire,
And compaignable, and bar hyrself so faire,
Syn thilke day that she was seven nyght oold,
That trewely she hath the herte in hoold
Of Chauntecleer, loken in every lith;
He loved hire so that wel was hym therwith.
But swich a joye was it to here hem synge,
Whan that the brighte sonne gan to sprynge,
In sweete accord, "My lief is faren in londe!"
For thilke tyme, as I have understonde,
Beestes and briddes koude speke and synge.

COCK-A-DOO

I love to hear the cock crow in
The middle of the day
It is an eerie sound in
The middle of the day
Sometimes it is a very hot day
Heavy for coming thunder
And the grass I tread on is dusty
And burnt yellow. Away
Over the river Bean which naturally
(It having been hot now for so long)
Runs shallow, stand up
The great yellow cornfields, but
Walking closely by the farm track
Not lifting my head, but foot by
Foot slowly, tired after a long
Walk, I see only the blue
And gray of the flint path, and
Each one of the particles of
Yellow dust on it. And this
Seeing, because of tiredness, becomes
A transfixion of seeing, more sharp
Than mirages are. Now comes the cry
Of the cock at midday
An eerie sound – cock-a-doooo – it
Sharpens a second time

The transfixion. If there were
A third sharpener
Coming this hot day with a butcher's edge
It would spell death.

WHAT DO WE GEESE WEAR FOR CLOTHES?

Oh, what do we geese wear for clothes?
   Gi, ga, gock!
We march out barefoot, day and night,
Dressed in featherwear of white,
   Gi, ga, gock!
We've only got one smock!

What do we geese eat for food?
   Gi, ga, gack!
Summertimes we pick the meadow;
Winters, farm wives keep us fed, oh,
   Gi, ga, gack!
Out of the oatmeal sack!

How do geese spend Martin's Mass?
   Gi, ga, geck!
Our keeper leads us from our pen
To Martin's schmaltzy feast and then,
   Gi, ga, geck!
It seems, they wring our neck!

GERMAN FOLK SONG
TRANSLATED BY W. D. SNODGRASS

THE REALM
OF AIR

THE EAGLE

He clasps the crag with crooked hands;
Close to the sun in lonely lands,
Ring'd with the azure world, he stands.

The wrinkled sea beneath him crawls;
He watches from his mountain walls,
And like a thunderbolt he falls.

WILD GEESE FLYING

Aware at first only of the dust of sound
  Drifting down to us here in the yard,
    I saw him look up, searching fathoms of air
      As for tidings,
        Some urgent spirits' honking aloft:
          Wild geese there – and my eyes strained after,
            Into that azure,
              Then, *there* they were: *there*,
                Flying in a straggle, so high, a wonder,
                  Glinting like wafers, silver fish-
                    Scales in the sun, a
                      Strewing of foil confetti, yet aimed;
                        The string of a kite's tail
                          Dipping, being drawn
                            Through that gulf stream of air
                              By their migrant passion; – at the edge
                                Of sight I still found them....
                                  Then, abruptly,
                                    Nowhere.

HUMMING-BIRD

I can imagine, in some otherworld
Primeval-dumb, far back
In that most awful stillness, that only gasped
    and hummed,
Humming-birds raced down the avenues.

Before anything had a soul,
While life was a heave of Matter, half inanimate,
This little bit chipped off in brilliance
And went whizzing through the slow, vast,
    succulent stems.

I believe there were no flowers then,
In the world where the humming-bird flashed
    ahead of creation.
I believe he pierced the slow vegetable veins with
    his long beak.

Probably he was big
As mosses, and little lizards, they say, were once big.
Probably he was a jabbing, terrifying monster.

We look at him through the wrong end of the long
    telescope of Time,
Luckily for us.

D. H. LAWRENCE
    51

THE BLUE SWALLOWS

Across the millstream below the bridge
Seven blue swallows divide the air
In shapes invisible and evanescent,
Kaleidoscopic beyond the mind's
Or memory's power to keep them there.

"History is where tensions were,"
"Form is the diagram of forces."
Thus, helplessly, there on the bridge,
While gazing down upon those birds —
How strange, to be above the birds! —
Thus helplessly the mind in its brain
Weaves up relation's spindrift web,
Seeing the swallows' tails as nibs
Dipped in invisible ink, writing . . .

Poor mind, what would you have them write?
Some cabalistic history
Whose authorship you might ascribe
To God? to Nature? Ah, poor ghost,
You've capitalized your Self enough.
That villainous William of Occam
Cut out the feet from under that dream
Some seven centuries ago.
It's taken that long for the mind

To waken, yawn and stretch, to see
With opened eyes emptied of speech
The real world where the spelling mind
Imposes with its grammar book
Unreal relations on the blue
Swallows. Perhaps when you will have
Fully awakened, I shall show you
A new thing: even the water
Flowing away beneath those birds
Will fail to reflect their flying forms,
And the eyes that see become as stones
Whence never tears shall fall again.

O swallows, swallows, poems are not
The point. Finding again the world,
That is the point, where loveliness
Adorns intelligible things
Because the mind's eye lit the sun.

SWIFTS

Fifteenth of May. Cherry blossom. The swifts
Materialize at the tip of a long scream
Of needle. "Look! They're back! Look!" And they're gone
On a steep

Controlled scream of skid
Round the house-end and away under the cherries. Gone.
Suddenly flickering in sky summit, three or four together,
Gnat-whisp frail, and hover-searching, and listening

For air-chills – are they too early? With a bowing
Power-thrust to left, then to right, then a flicker they
Tilt into a slide, a tremble for balance,
Then a lashing down disappearance

Behind elms.
                    They've made it again,
Which means the globe's still working, the Creation's
Still waking refreshed, our summer's
Still all to come –
                    And here they are, here they are again
Erupting across yard stones
Shrapnel-scatter terror. Frog-gapers,
Speedway goggles, international mobsters –

A bolas of three or four wire screams
Jockeying across each other
On their switchback wheel of death.
They swat past, hard-fletched,

Veer on the hard air, toss up over the roof,
And are gone again. Their mole-dark laboring,
Their lunatic limber scramming frenzy
And their whirling blades

Sparkle out into blue –
                    Not ours any more.
Rats ransacked their nests so now they shun us.
Round luckier houses now
They crowd their evening dirt-track meetings,

Racing their discords, screaming as if speed-burned,
Head-height, clipping the doorway
With their leaden velocity and their butterfly lightness,
Their too much power, their arrow-thwack into the eaves.

Every year a first-fling, nearly-flying
Misfit flopped in our yard,
Groggily somersaulting to get airborne.
He bat-crawled on his tiny useless feet, tangling his flails

Like a broken toy, and shrieking thinly
Till I tossed him up – then suddenly he flowed away under
His bowed shoulders of enormous swimming power,
Slid away along levels wobbling

On the fine wire they have reduced life to,
And crashed among the raspberries.
Then followed fiery hospital hours
In a kitchen. The mustached goblin savage

Nested in a scarf. The bright blank
Blind, like an angel, to my meat-crumbs and flies.
Then eyelids resting. Wasted clingers curled.
The inevitable balsa death.

                    Finally burial

For the husk
Of my little Apollo –

The charred scream
Folded in its huge power.

THE KINGFISHER

In a year the nightingales were said to be so loud
they drowned out slumber, and peafowl strolled
        screaming
beside the ruined nunnery, through the long evening
of a dazzled pub crawl, the halcyon color, portholed
by those eye-spots' stunning tapestry, unsettled
the pastoral nightfall with amazements opening.

Months later, intermission in a pub on
        Fifty-fifth Street
found one of them still breathless, the other quizzical,
acting the philistine, puncturing Stravinsky – "Tell
me, what *was* that racket in the orchestra about?" –
hauling down the Firebird, harum-scarum, like a kite,
a burnished, breathing wreck that didn't hurt at all.

Among the Bronx Zoo's exiled jungle fowl, they heard
through headphones of a separating panic, the bellbird
reiterate its single *chong*, a scream nobody answered.
When he mourned, "The poetry is gone," she quailed,
seeing how his hands shook, sobered into feeling old.
By midnight, yet another fifth would have been killed.

A Sunday morning, the November of their cataclysm
(Dylan Thomas brought in *in extremis* to St. Vincent's,

that same week, a symptomatic datum) found them
wandering a downtown churchyard. Among
    its headstones,
while from unruined choirs the noise of Christendom
poured over Wall Street, a benison in vestments,

a late thrush paused, in transit from some grizzled
spruce bog to the humid equatorial fireside: berry-
eyed, bark-brown above, with dark hints of trauma
in the stigmata of its underparts – or so, too bruised
just then to have invented anything so fancy,
later, re-embroidering a retrospect, she had supposed.

In gray England, years of muted recrimination (then
dead silence) later, she could not have said how many
spoiled takeoffs, how many entanglements gone
    sodden,
how many gaudy evenings made frantic by just one
insomniac nightingale, how many liaisons gone down
screaming in a stroll beside the ruined nunnery;

a kingfisher's burnished plunge, the color
of felicity afire, came glancing like an arrow
through landscapes of untended memory: ardor
illuminating with its terrifying currency
now no mere glimpse, no porthole vista
but, down on down, the uninhabitable sorrow.

FIELD AND
FOREST

THE CUCKOO SONG

    Sing, cuccu, nu. Sing, cuccu.
    Sing, cuccu. Sing, cuccu, nu.

Sumer is i-cumen in –
   Lhude sing, cuccu!
Groweth sed and bloweth med
   And springth the wude nu.
      Sing, cuccu!

Awe bleteth after lomb,
   Lhouth after calve cu,
Bulluc sterteth, bucke verteth –
   Murie sing, cuccu!
     Cuccu, cuccu.
   Wel singes thu, cuccu.
   Ne swik thu naver nu!

THE MERRY CUCKOO

The merry Cuckow, messenger of Spring,
   His trompet shrill hath thrise already sounded:
    that warnes al louers wayt vpon their king,
   who now is comming forth with girland crouned.
With noyse whereof the quyre of Byrds resounded
   their anthemes sweet devized of loues prayse,
   that all the woods theyr ecchoes back rebounded,
   as if they knew the meaning of their layes.
But mongst them all, which did Loues honor rayse
   no word was heard of her that most it ought,
   but she his precept proudly disobayes,
   and doth his ydle message set at nought.
Therefore O loue, vnlesse she turne to thee
   ere Cuckow end, let her a rebell be.

THE LARK

Swift through the yielding air I glide,
While nights shall be shades, I abide,
Yet in my flight (though ne'er so fast)
I tune and time the wild wind's blast;
And e'er the sun be come about,
Teach the young lark his lesson out;
Who, early as the day is born,
Sings his shrill anthem to the rising morn.

Let never mortal lose the pains
To imitate my airy strains,
Whose pitch, too high for human ears,
Was set me by the tuneful spheres.
I carol to the Fairies' King,
Wake him a-mornings when I sing,
And when the sun stoops to the deep,
Rock him again, and his fair Queen to sleep.

ANON.

QUAIL IN AUTUMN

Autumn has turned the dark trees toward the hill;
The wind has ceased; the air is white and chill.
Red leaves no longer dance against your foot,
The branch reverts to tree, the tree to root.

And now in this bare place your step will find
A twig that snaps flintlike against the mind;
Then thundering above your giddy head,
Small quail dart up, through shafting sunlight fled.

Like brightness buried by one's sullen mood
The quail rise startled from the threadbare wood;
A voice, a step, a swift sun-thrust of feather
And earth and air come properly together.

THE HOLLOW WOOD

Out in the sun the goldfinch flits
Along the thistle-tops, flits and twits
Above the hollow wood
Where birds swim like fish –
Fish that laugh and shriek –
To and fro, far below
In the pale hollow wood.

Lichen, ivy, and moss
Keep evergreen the trees
That stand half-flayed and dying,
And the dead trees on their knees
In dog's-mercury and moss:
And the bright twit of the goldfinch drops
Down there as he flits on thistle-tops.

TO THE WOODLARK

O stay, sweet warbling woodlark, stay,
Nor quit for me the trembling spray;
A hapless lover courts thy lay,
    Thy soothing fond complaining.

Again, again that tender part,
That I may catch thy melting art;
For surely that wad touch her heart,
    Wha kills me wi' disdaining.

Say, was thy little mate unkind,
And heard thee as the careless wind?
Oh, nocht but love and sorrow join'd
    Sic notes o' wae could wauken.

Thou tells o' never-ending care,
O' speechless grief, and dark despair;
For pity's sake, sweet bird, nae mair!
    Or my poor heart is broken!

WOODPECKER

Suddenly, like an arrow from the East,
Smart as new paint appeared our gorgeous guest,
Green in his plumage, scarlet on his crown,
Strolling about a tree-trunk upsidedown,
Tap-tapping busily with beak on bark,
His mind imagineless, his purpose dark
To us who watched him, startled out of speech,
Exchanging secret glances each with each.
So all that day, being young and fearing not
Lest custom dull the treasure we had got,
All that day long we jingled, as we went,
New-minted coins of bright astonishment.

GERALD BULLETT   67

A WHIPPOORWILL IN THE WOODS

Night after night, it was very nearly enough,
they said, to drive you crazy: a whippoorwill
in the woods repeating itself like the stuck groove
of an LP with a defect, and no way possible
        of turning the thing off.

And night after night, they said, in the insomniac
small hours the whipsawing voice of obsession
would have come in closer, the way a sick
thing does when it's done for – or maybe the reason
        was nothing more melodramatic

than a night-flying congregation of moths, lured in
in their turn by house-glow, the strange heat
of it – imagine the nebular dangerousness, if one
were a moth, the dark pockmarked with beaks, the great
        dim shapes, the bright extinction –

if moths are indeed, after all, what a whippoorwill
favors. Who knows? Anyhow, from one point of view
insects are to be seen as an ailment, moths above all:
the filmed-over, innumerable nodes of spun-out tissue
        untidying the trees, the larval

spew of such hairy hordes, one wonders what use
they can be other than as a guarantee no bird

goes hungry. We're like that. The webbiness,
the gregariousness of the many are what we can't abide.
         We single out for notice

above all what's disjunct, the way birds are,
with their unhooked-up, cheekily anarchic
dartings and flashings, their uncalled-for color –
the indelible look of the rose-breasted grosbeak
         an aunt of mine, a noticer

of such things before the noticing had or needed
a name, drew my five-year-old attention up to, in
the green deeps of a maple. She never married,
believed her cat had learned to leave birds alone,
         and for years, node after node,

by lingering degrees she made way within for
what wasn't so much a thing as it was a system,
a webwork of error that throve until it killed her.
What is health? We must all die sometime.
         Whatever it is, out there

in the woods, that begins to seem like
a species of madness, we survive as we can:
the hooked-up, the humdrum, the brief, tragic
wonder of being at all. The whippoorwill out in
         the woods, for me, brought back

as by a relay, from a place at such a distance
no recollection now in place could reach so far,
the memory of a memory she told me of once:
of how her father, my grandfather, by whatever
        now unfathomable happenstance,

carried her (she might have been five) into the
        breathing night.
"Listen!" she said he'd said. "Did you hear it?
That was a whippoorwill." And she (and I) never
        forgot.

BLACK COCKATOOS

Each certain kind of weather or of light
has its own creatures. Somewhere else they wait
as though they but inhabited heat or cold,
twilight or dawn, and knew no other state.
Then at their time they come, timid or bold.

So when the long drought-winds, sandpaper-harsh,
were still, and the air changed, and the clouds came,
and other birds were quiet in prayer or fear,
these knew their hour. Before the first far flash
lit up, or the first thunder spoke its name,
in heavy flight they came, till I could hear
the wild black cockatoos, tossed on the crest
of their high trees, crying the world's unrest.

THE CRANES

The western wind has blown but a few days;
Yet the first leaf already flies from the bough.
On the drying paths I walk in my thin shoes;
In the first cold I have donned my quilted coat.
Through shallow ditches the floods are clearing away;
Through sparse bamboos trickles a slanting light.
In the early dusk, down an alley of green moss,
The garden-boy is leading the cranes home.

TRANSLATED BY ARTHUR WALEY

AT
WATER'S EDGE

A GULL GOES UP

Gulls when they fly move in a liquid arc,
Still head, and wings that bend above the breast,
Covering its glitter with a cloak of dark,
Gulls fly. So as at last toward balm and rest,
Remembering wings, the desperate leave their earth,
Bear from their earth what there was ruinous-crossed,
Peace from distress, and love from nothing-worth,
Fast at the heart, its jewels of dear cost.
Gulls go up hushed to that entrancing flight,
With never a feather of all the body stirred.
So in an air less rare than longing might
The dream of flying lift a marble bird.
Desire it is that flies; then wings are freight
That only bear the feathered heart no weight.

SEAGULLS

A gull, up close,
looks surprisingly stuffed.
His fluffy chest seems filled
with an inexpensive taxidermist's material
rather lumpily inserted. The legs,
unbent, are childish crayon strokes –
too simple to be workable.
And even the feather-markings,
whose intricate symmetry is the usual glory of birds,
are in the gull slovenly,
as if God makes too many
to make them very well.

Are they intelligent?
We imagine so, because they are ugly.
The sardonic one-eyed profile, slightly cross,
the narrow, ectomorphic head, badly combed,
the wide and nervous and well-muscled rump
all suggest deskwork: shipping rates
by day, Schopenhauer
by night, and endless coffee.

At that hour on the beach
when the flies begin biting in the renewed coolness
and the backsliding skin of the after-surf

reflects a pink shimmer before being blotted,
the gulls stand around in the dimpled sand
like those melancholy European crowds
that gather in cobbled public squares in the wake
of assassinations and invasions,
heads cocked to hear the latest radio reports.

It is also this hour when plump young couples
walk down to the water, bumping together,
and stand thigh-deep in the rhythmic glass.
Then they walk back toward the car,
tugging as if at a secret between them,
but which neither quite knows –
walk capricious paths through the scattering gulls,
as in some mythologies
beautiful gods stroll unconcerned
among our mortal apprehensions.

THE HERON

The heron stands in water where the swamp
Has deepened to the blackness of a pool,
Or balances with one leg on a hump
Of marsh grass heaped above a musk-rat hole.

He walks the shallow with an antic grace.
The great feet break the ridges of the sand,
The long eye notes the minnow's hiding place.
His beak is quicker than a human hand.

He jerks a frog across his bony lip,
Then points his heavy bill above the wood.
The wide wings flap but once to lift him up.
A single ripple starts from where he stood.

THE GRAY HERON

It held its head still
while its body and green
legs wobbled in wide arcs
from side to side. When
it stalked out of sight,
I went after it, but all
I could find where I was
expecting to see the bird
was a three-foot-long lizard
in ill-fitting skin
and with linear mouth
expressive of the even temper
of the mineral kingdom.
It stopped and tilted its head,
which was much like
a fieldstone with an eye
in it, which was watching me
to see if I would go
or change into something else.

CORMORANTS

those perennial apparitions
of the backwaters – their shadows
the faded sails of anchored boats

SANDPIPER

The roaring alongside he takes for granted,
and that every so often the world is bound to shake.
He runs, he runs to the south, finical, awkward,
in a state of controlled panic, a student of Blake.

The beach hisses like fat. On his left, a sheet
of interrupting water comes and goes
and glazes over his dark and brittle feet.
He runs, he runs straight through it, watching his toes.

– Watching, rather, the spaces of sand between them,
where (no detail too small) the Atlantic drains
rapidly backwards and downwards. As he runs,
he stares at the dragging grains.

The world is a mist. And then the world is
minute and vast and clear. The tide
is higher or lower. He couldn't tell you which.
His beak is focussed; he is preoccupied,

looking for something, something, something.
Poor bird, he is obsessed!
The millions of grains are black, white, tan, and gray,
mixed with quartz grains, rose and amethyst.

CURLEWS LIFT

Out of the maternal watery blue lines

Stripped of all but their cry
Some twists of near-inedible sinew

They slough off
The robes of bilberry blue
The cloud-stained bogland

They veer up and eddy away over
The stone horns

They trail a long, dangling, falling aim
Across water

Lancing their voices
Through the skin of this light

Drinking the nameless and naked
Through trembling bills

THE FLAMINGOS
Jardin des Plantes, Paris

With all the subtle paints of Fragonard
no more of their red and white could be expressed
than someone would convey about his mistress
by telling you, "She was lovely, lying there

still soft with sleep." They rise above the green
grass and lightly sway on their long pink stems,
side by side, like enormous feathery blossoms,
seducing (more seductively than Phryne)

themselves; till, necks curling, they sink their large
pale eyes into the softness of their down,
where apple-red and jet-black lie concealed.

A shriek of envy shakes the parrot cage;
but *they* stretch out, astonished, and one by one
stride into their imaginary world.

RAINER MARIA RILKE   83
TRANSLATED BY STEPHEN MITCHELL

ONE OF THE STRANGEST

Stuffed pink stocking, the neck,
toe of pointed black, the angled beak,
thick heel with round eye in it upside down, the pate,

swivels, dabbles, skims the soup of pond all day
for small meat. That split polished toe is mouth
of the wading flamingo

whose stilts, the rosy knee joints, bend
the wrong way. When planted
on one straight stem, a big fluffy flower

is body a pink leg, wrung, lifts up over,
lays an awkward shoe to sleep on top of,
between flocculent elbows, the soft peony wings.

PELICANS

Funnel-web spider, snake and octopus,
pitcher-plant and vampire-bat and shark –
these are cold water on an easy faith.
Look at them, but don't linger.
If we stare too long, something looks back at us;
something gazes through from underneath;
something crooks a very dreadful finger
down there in an unforgotten dark.

Turn away then, and look up at the sky.
There sails that old clever Noah's Ark,
the well-turned, well-carved pelican
with his wise comic eye;
he turns and wheels down, kind as an
　　　ambulance-driver,
to join his fleet. Pelicans rock together,
solemn as clowns in white on a circus-river,
meaning: this world holds every sort of weather.

JUDITH WRIGHT

THE LOON UPON THE LAKE

I looked across the water,
    I bent o'er it and listened,
I thought it was my lover,
    My true lover's paddle glistened.
Joyous thus his light canoe would the silver ripples
    wake.
But no! – it is the loon alone – the loon upon the lake.
Ah me! it is the loon alone – the loon upon the lake.

I see the fallen maple
    Where he stood, his red scarf waving,
Though waters nearly bury
    Boughs they then were newly laving.
I hear his last farewell, as it echoed from the brake. –
But no, it is the loon alone – the loon upon the lake,
Ah me! it is the loon alone – the loon upon the lake.

BIRDS OF PREY

THE TWA CORBIES

As I was walking all alane,
I heard twa corbies making a mane;
The tane unto the t'other say,
"Where sall we gang and dine to-day?"

"In behint yon auld fail dyke,
I wot there lies a new slain knight;
And naebody kens that he lies there,
But his hawk, his hound, and lady fair.

"His hound is to the hunting gane,
His hawk to fetch the wild-fowl hame,
His lady's ta'en another mate,
So we may mak our dinner sweet.

"Ye'll sit on his white hause bane,
And I'll pike out his bonny blue een;
Wi ae lock o his gowden hair
We'll theek our nest when it grows bare.

"Mony a one for him makes mane,
But nane sall ken where he is gane;
Oer his white banes, when they are bare,
The wind sal blaw for evermair."

ANON.   89

VULTURES

Hung there in the thermal
whiteout of noon, dark ash
in the chimney's updraft, turning
slowly like a thumb pressed down
on target; indolent V's; flies, until they drop.

Then they're hyenas, raucous
around the kill, flapping their black
umbrellas, the feathered red-eyed widows
whose pot bodies violate mourning,
the snigger at funerals,
the burp at the wake.

They cluster, like beetles
laying their eggs on carrion,
gluttonous for a space, a little
territory of murder: food
and children.

Frowzy old saint, bald-
headed and musty, scrawny-
necked recluse on your pillar
of blazing air which is not
heaven: what do you make
of death, which you do not
cause, which you eat daily?

I make life, which is a prayer.
I make clean bones.
I make a gray zinc noise
which to me is a song.

Well, heart, out of all this
carnage, could you do better?

MARGARET ATWOOD   91

THE VULTURE

The Vulture eats between his meals,
And that's the reason why
He very, very rarely feels
As well as you and I.

His eye is dull, his head is bald,
His neck is growing thinner.
Oh! what a lesson for us all
To only eat at dinner!

VULTURE

The vulture's very like a sack
   Set down and left there drooping.
His crooked neck and creaky back
   Look badly bent from stooping
Down to the ground to eat dead cows
   So they won't go to waste
Thus making up in usefulness
   For what he lacks in taste.

EGYPTIAN KITES

Verminous aeronaut, leaflight turkey, kite,
smothering an airpuff with heave of shoulder, fingering
delicately with stretched flight plumes your sky,
    or crucified
in calm you float, wheeling symbol of an old world
in the reeling blue serene, looking for something dead.

On ground the owl is grand, the sparrow cheeky,
the hoopoe decent, but you, with your sardine tail,
on earth so dusty, so bedraggled and lousy,
mean, musty, cumbersome, with beastly tastes,
seem cruel and cowardly in gestures of your snaky head.

Yes, for air is the arena of the carnal kite;
flat seas for floating there, and current for the cruise;
in intense glare and blaze going like ghosts,
twittering high and mewing above our haze,
moths to the molten sun they eye our earth for dirt.

Brown kite, I saw you in the mating season moved,
coarse-bodied powerful scavenger, hurling with
    your hook
of beak to the yellow grip of the beak of your mate,
and so in jostle of joy come falling falling,
unbalanced bird-flesh, till you reached the river Nile.

Then slow with flap of wing, steadying with screw
        driver tail,
huge over the mud, ascending among shining sails,
you each went your own way, and, tier upon tier in the air,
others kept up their high tittering in sunny stations,
feeling the air with feathers, poised in the plunge
        of the sun.

FLIGHTLESS
BIRDS

THE WING OF THE OSTRICH
REJOICETH

The wing of the ostrich rejoiceth;
But are her pinions and feathers kindly?
For she leaveth her eggs on the earth,
And warmeth them in the dust,
And forgetteth that the foot may crush them,
Or that the wild beast may trample them.
She is hardened against her young ones,
     as if they were not hers:
Though her labour be in vain, she is without fear;
Because God hath deprived her of wisdom,
Neither hath he imparted to her understanding.
What time she lifteth up herself on high,
She scorneth the horse and his rider.

HE "DIGESTETH HARDE YRON"

Although the aepyornis
   or roc that lived in Madagascar, and
the moa are extinct,
the camel-sparrow, linked
   with them in size – the large sparrow
Xenophon saw walking by a stream – was and is
a symbol of justice.

This bird watches his chicks with
   a maternal concentration – and he's
been mothering the eggs
at night six weeks – his legs
   their only weapon of defense.
He is swifter than a horse; he has a foot hard
as a hoof; the leopard

is not more suspicious. How
   could he, prized for plumes and eggs and young,
used even as a riding-beast, respect men
   hiding actor-like in ostrich skins, with the right hand
making the neck move as if alive
and from a bag the left hand strewing grain, that
     ostriches

might be decoyed and killed! Yes, this is he
whose plume was anciently
the plume of justice; he
    whose comic duckling head on its
great neck revolves with compass-needle nervousness
when he stands guard,

    in S-like foragings as he is
    preening the down on his leaden-skinned back.
The egg piously shown
as Leda's very own
    from which Castor and Pollux hatched,
was an ostrich-egg. And what could have been more fit
for the Chinese lawn it

    grazed on as a gift to an
    emperor who admired strange birds, than this
one, who builds his mud-made
nest in dust yet will wade
    in lake or sea till only the head shows.

            .   .   .   .   .   .

    Six hundred ostrich-brains served
        at one banquet, the ostrich-plume-tipped tent
    and desert spear, jewel-
    gorgeous ugly egg-shell

    goblets, eight pairs of ostriches
in harness, dramatize a meaning
always missed by the externalist.

    The power of the visible
    is the invisible; as even where
no tree of freedom grows,
so-called brute courage knows.
    Heroism is exhausting, yet
it contradicts a greed that did not wisely spare
the harmless solitaire

    or great auk in its grandeur;
    unsolicitude having swallowed up
all giant birds but an alert gargantuan
    little-winged, magnificently speedy running-bird.
This one remaining rebel
is the sparrow-camel.

IF I WERE A CASSOWARY

If I were a cassowary
On the plains of Timbuctoo,
I would eat a missionary,
Cassock, bands, and hymn-book too.

THE
NIGHTINGALE

TO THE NIGHTINGALE

O Nightingale, that on yon bloomy Spray
Warbl'st at eeve, when all the woods are still,
Thou with fresh hope the Lovers heart dost fill,
While the jolly hours lead on propitious *May*,
Thy liquid notes that close the eye of Day,
First heard before the shallow Cuccoo's bill
Portend success in love; O if *Jove's* will
Have linkt that amorous power to thy soft lay,
Now timely sing, ere the rude Bird of Hate
Foretell my hopeless doom in som Grove ny:
As thou from yeer to yeer hast sung too late
For my relief; yet hadst no reason why,
Whether the Muse, or Love call thee his mate,
Both them I serve, and of their train am I.

TO A NIGHTINGALE

Sweet Bird, that sing'st away the early Hours,
Of Winters past, or coming, void of Care,
Well pleasèd with Delights which present are,
Fair seasons, budding Sprays, sweet-smelling Flow'rs.
To Rocks, to Springs, to Rills, from leavy Bow'rs,
Thou thy Creator's Goodness dost declare,
And what dear Gifts on thee he did not spare,
A Stain to human Sense in Sin that low'rs.
What Soul can be so sick, which by thy Songs
(Attir'd in sweetness) sweetly is not driven
Quite to forget Earth's Turmoils, Spites and Wrongs,
And lift a reverend Eye and Thought to Heaven?
Sweet, artless Songster, thou my Mind doest raise
To Ayres of Spheres, yea, and to Angels' Layes.

THE NIGHTINGALES
from Prometheus Unbound

There the voluptuous nightingales,
Are awake through all the broad noon-day,
When one with bliss or sadness fails,
And through the windless ivy-boughs,
Sick with sweet love, droops dying away
On its mate's music-panting bosom;
Another from the swinging blossom,
Watching to catch the languid close
Of the last strain, then lifts on high
The wings of the weak melody,
Till some new strain of feeling bear
The song, and all the woods are mute;
When there is heard through the dim air
The rush of wings, and rising there
Like many a lake-surrounded flute,
Sounds overflow the listener's brain
So sweet that joy is almost pain.

PHILOMELA

Hark! ah the Nightingale!
    The tawny-throated!
Hark! from that moonlit cedar what a burst!
    What triumph! hark – what pain!

    O Wanderer from a Grecian shore,
Still, after many years, in distant lands,
Still nourishing in thy bewilder'd brain
That wild, unquench'd, deep-sunken, old-world pain –
    Say, will it never heal?
    And can this fragrant lawn
    With its cool trees, and night,
    And the sweet tranquil Thames,
    And moonshine, and the dew,
    To thy rack'd heart and brain
    Afford no balm?

    Dost thou to-night behold
Here, through the moonlight on this English grass,
The unfriendly palace in the Thracian wild?
    Dost thou again peruse
    With hot cheeks and sear'd eyes
The too clear web, and thy dumb Sister's shame?
    Dost thou once more assay
    Thy flight, and feel come over thee,

Poor Fugitive, the feathery change
Once more, and once more seem to make resound
With love and hate, triumph and agony,
Lone Daulis, and the high Cephissian vale?
       Listen, Eugenia –

How thick the bursts come crowding through
    the leaves!
      Again – thou hearest!
       Eternal Passion!
       Eternal Pain!

PAIN OR JOY

> Hark! that's the nightingale,
> Telling the selfsame tale
Her song told when this ancient earth was young:
So echoes answered when her song was sung
> In the first wooded vale.

> We call it love and pain
> The passion of her strain;
And yet we little understand or know;
Why should it not be rather joy that so
> Throbs in each throbbing vein?

THE
PEACOCK

I SAW A PEACOCK

I saw a peacock with a fiery tail
I saw a blazing comet drop down hail
I saw a cloud with ivy circled round
I saw a sturdy oak creep on the ground
I saw a pismire swallow up a whale
I saw a raging sea brim full of ale
I saw a Venice glass sixteen foot deep
I saw a well full of men's tears that weep
I saw their eyes all in a flame of fire
I saw a house as big as the moon and higher
I saw the sun even in the midst of night
I saw the Man that saw this wondrous sight.

ANON.

ON A PEACOCK

Thou foolish Bird, of Feathers proud,
Whose Lustre yet thine Eyes ne're see:
The gazing Wonder of the Crowd,
Beauteous, not to thy self, but Me!
Thy Hellish Voice doth those affright,
Whose Eyes were charmed at thy sight.

Vainly thou think'st, those Eyes of thine
Were such as sleepy *Argus* lost;
When he was touch'd with rod Divine,
Who lat of Vigilance did boast.
Little at best they'll thee avail,
Not in thine *Head*, but in thy *Tayl*.

Wisemen do *forward* look to try
What will in *following* Moments come:
Backward thy useless Eyes do ly,
Nor do enquire of *future* doom.
"Nothing can remedy what's past;
Wisedom must guard the present cast."

Our Eyes are best employ'd at home,
Not when they are on others plac'd:
From thine but little good can come,
Which never on thy self are cast:
What can of such a Tool be made:
A Tayl *well-furnish'd*, but an empty Head.

THE PEACOCK'S EYE

Mark you how the peacock's eye
Winks away its ring of green,
Barter'd for an azure dye,
And the piece that's like a bean,
The pupil, plays its liquid jet
To win a look of violet.

DOMINATION OF BLACK

At night, by the fire,
The colors of the bushes
And of the fallen leaves,
Repeating themselves,
Turned in the room,
Like the leaves themselves
Turning in the wind.
Yes: but the color of the heavy hemlocks
Came striding.
And I remembered the cry of the peacocks.

The colors of their tails
Were like the leaves themselves
Turning in the wind,
In the twilight wind.
They swept over the room,
Just as they flew from the boughs of the hemlocks
Down to the ground.
I heard them cry – the peacocks.
Was it a cry against the twilight
Or against the leaves themselves
Turning in the wind,
Turning as the flames
Turned in the fire,
Turning as the tails of the peacocks

Turned in the loud fire,
Loud as the hemlocks
Full of the cry of the peacocks?
Or was it a cry against the hemlocks?

Out of the window,
I saw how the planets gathered
Like the leaves themselves
Turning in the wind.
I saw how the night came,
Came striding like the color of the heavy hemlocks
I felt afraid.
And I remembered the cry of the peacocks.

THE PEACOCK

I speak to the unbeautiful of this bird
    Celestially bored,
That on gnarled gray feet under willows trails
Too much of himself, like Proust, a long brocade
Along, not seen but felt; that's never spared,
    Most mortal of his trials,
  Lifting this burden up in pride.

The outspread tail is drab seen from the back
    But it's worthwhile to look
At what strenuous midribs make the plumage stretch.
Then, while it teeters in the light wind, ah
He turns, black, buff, green, gold, that zodiac
    Of – no, not eyes so much
  As idiot mouths repeating: I.

Consider other birds: the murderous swan
    And dodo now undone,
The appalling dove, hens' petulant sisterhood;
And now this profile that no cry alarms,
Tense with idlesse, as though already on
    A terrace in boxwood
  Or graven in a coat of arms;

And in all these, the comic flaw of nature
    No natural hand can suture,
A lessening – whether by want of shape they fail,
Of song, or will to live, or something else.
How comforting to think blest any creature
    So vain, so beautiful!
  But some have known such comfort false.

A beatitude of trees which shall inherit
    Whoever's poor in spirit
Receives the peacock into cumbersome shade.
Some who have perfect beauty do not grieve,
As I, when beauty passes. They've known merit
    In word, emotion, deed:
  Lone angels round each human grave.

PEACOCK DISPLAY

He approaches her, trailing his whole fortune,
Perfectly cocksure, and suddenly spreads
The huge fan of his tail for her amazement.

Each turquoise and purple, black-horned,
    walleyed quill
Comes quivering forward, an amphitheatric shell
For his most fortunate audience: her alone.

He plumes himself. He shakes his brassily gold
Wings and rump in a dance, lifting his claws
Stiff-legged under the great bulge of his breast.

And she strolls calmly away, pecking and pausing,
Not watching him, astonished to discover
All these seeds spread just for her in the dirt.

THE OWL

THE OWL

OWLS

Under black yews that protect them
    the owls perch in a row
like alien gods whose red eyes
    glitter. They meditate.

Petrified, they will perch there till
    the melancholy hour
when the slanting sun is ousted,
    and darkness settles down.

    From their posture, the wise
learn to shun, in this world at least,
    motion and commotion;

impassioned by passing shadows,
    man will always be scourged
for trying to change his place.

CHARLES BAUDELAIRE   125
TRANSLATED BY RICHARD HOWARD

THE OWL

Owl of the wildwood I:
Muffled in sleep I drowse,
Where no fierce sun in heaven
Can me arouse.

My haunt's a hollow
In a half-dead tree,
Whose strangling ivy
Shields and shelters me.

But when dark's starlight
Thrids my green domain,
My plumage trembles and stirs,
I wake again:

A spectral moon
Silvers the world I see;
Out of their daylong lairs
Creep thievishly

Night's living things.
Then I,
Wafted away on soundless pinions
Fly;
Curdling her arches
With my hunting-cry:

A-hooh! a-hooh:
Four notes; and then,
Solemn, sepulchral, cold,
Four notes again,
The listening dingles
Of my woodland through:
A-hooh! A-hooh!
   A-hooh!

THE OWL

Downhill I came, hungry, and yet not starved;
Cold, yet had heat within me that was proof
Against the North wind; tired, yet so that rest
Had seemed the sweetest thing under a roof.

Then at the inn I had food, fire, and rest,
Knowing how hungry, cold, and tired was I.
All of the night was quite barred out except
An owl's cry, a most melancholy cry

Shaken out long and clear upon the hill,
No merry note, nor cause of merriment,
But one telling me plain what I escaped
And others could not, that night, as in I went.

And salted was my food, and my repose,
Salted and sobered, too, by the bird's voice
Speaking for all who lay under the stars,
Soldiers and poor, unable to rejoice.

OWL

Clocks belled twelve. Main Street showed otherwise
Than its suburb of woods: nimbus-
Lit, but unpeopled, held its windows
Of wedding pastries,

Diamond rings, potted roses, fox-skins
Ruddy on the wax mannequins
In a glassed tableau of affluence.
From deep-sunk basements

What moved the pale, raptorial owl
Then, to squall above the level
Of streetlights and wires, its wall to wall
Wingspread in control

Of the ferrying currents, belly
Dense-feathered, fearfully soft to
Look upon? Rats' teeth gut the city
Shaken by owl cry.

OWL

Now that the owl-light – in the time between
Dog and wolf, as some call it – ends, we wait
    As you alight on an unseen
        Branch to interrogate

The listener and the rememberer;
Lost outlines heighten – as last colors fade –
    The sounder darkness you confer
        Upon the spruce's shade.

Deluded by the noonlight's wide display
Of everything, our vision floats through thin
    Spaces of ill-illumined day:
        How we are taken in

By what we take in with our roving eyes!
Your constant ones, if moved to track or trace,
    Take their head with them, lantern-wise
        Taking heed, keeping face

In the society of night, and keeping
Faith with the spirit of pure fixity
    That sets the mind's great heart to leaping
        At what you more than see.

Medusa's visage gazed our bodies to
Literal stone unshaded: your face, caught
   In our glance widely eyes us through,
     Astonishing our thought.

You who debated with the nightingale
The rectitude of northern wisdom, cold
   Against the love-stuff of the tale
     The laid-back south had told;

And yet who stood amid the lovely, thick
Leaves of the ivy, while in all their folly
   The larks and thrushes sought the prick
     And berries of the holly;

You who confounded the rapacious crow
Thus to be favored by the great sky-eyed
   Queen of the air and all who know,
     Now ever by her side;

With silent wing and interrogative
Cry in lieu of a merely charming song,
   You sound the dark in which you live
     Perched above right and wrong.

Resonance is not vacancy: although
He could hear nothing in your hollow howls

But woe and his own guilt, Thoreau
　　Rejoiced that there were owls.

Scattered and occasional questionings
With here and there too late a warning shout,
　　Wisdom arises on the wings
　　　　Of darkness and of doubt.

Where in day's vastnesses does truth reside?
In noon's uncompromising light and heat
　　When even our own shadows hide
　　　　Under our very feet?

Or in the hidden center of the quick
Resilient dark on which your narrowed sight
　　So pointedly alights to pick
　　　　Not the day, but the night,

Its fruitful flower, petaled a hundredfold?
Oh it is there, truth, with the poor blind prey
　　Trembling with prescience or cold
　　　　Waiting for how your way

Of well-tuned suddenness and certitude
Tight-strung and execution highly wrought
　　Leads to the pounced-on object, food
　　　　For something beyond thought,

By overlooking nothing, overseeing
In all the stillness hidden, tiny motions
   Squirming with the life of being
      Inferences and notions.

With patient agency the beak and claws
Of fierce sublime awareness pluck it clean
   Deriving what for us are laws
      Governing the unseen.

Under torn canvas we put out to sea
Trusting, though puzzled by what glows above,
   To something like philosophy
      To be the helmsman of

Life (but whose life?). Your lessons of the land,
Down-to-tree, then, if not -to-earth, indict
   Our helplessness to understand
      Just what we are at night.

Immensities of starlight told us lies
Of what and where we are; but, we allow,
   Drunk with the Milky Way, our eyes
      Are on the Wagon now,

Fugitive slaves, leaving despair for dread
As if in search of the cold, freeing North,

> *Keep gazing steadily ahead*
> *Keep on Keep knowing forth*

You urge us, as your silences address
The power that Minerva chose you for:
    Great-winged, far-ranging consciousness
      Now come to rest in your

Olympian attentiveness that finds
The affrighted heartbeat on the ground, perceives
    The flutter of substances, the mind's
      Life in the fallen leaves.

THE HAWK

THE MAN-OF-WAR HAWK

Yon black man-of-war hawk that wheels in the light
Over the black ship's white sky-s'l, sunned cloud
    to the sight,
Have we low-flyers wings to ascend to his height?

No arrow can reach him; nor thought can attain
To the placid supreme in the sweep of his reign.

HERMAN MELVILLE

HAWK ROOSTING

I sit in the top of the wood, my eyes closed.
Inaction, no falsifying dream
Between my hooked head and hooked feet:
Or in sleep rehearse perfect kills and eat.

The convenience of the high trees!
The air's buoyancy and the sun's ray
Are of advantage to me;
And the earth's face upward for my inspection.

My feet are locked upon the rough bark.
It took the whole of Creation
To produce my foot, my each feather:
Now I hold Creation in my foot

Or fly up, and revolve it all slowly –
I kill where I please because it is all mine.
There is no sophistry in my body:
My manners are tearing off heads –

The allotment of death.
For the one path of my flight is direct
Through the bones of the living.
No arguments assert my right:

The sun is behind me.
Nothing has changed since I began.
My eye has permitted no change.
I am going to keep things like this.

EVENING HAWK

From plane of light to plane, wings dipping through
Geometries and orchids that the sunset builds,
Out of the peak's black angularity of shadow, riding
The last tumultuous avalanche of
Light above pines and the guttural gorge,
The hawk comes.

        His wing
Scythes down another day, his motion
Is that of the honed steel-edge, we hear
The crashless fall of stalks of Time.

The head of each stalk is heavy with the gold of our error.

Look! look! he is climbing the last light
Who knows neither Time nor error, and under
Whose eye, unforgiving, the world, unforgiven, swings
Into shadow.

        Long now,
The last thrush is still, the last bat
Now cruises in his sharp hieroglyphics. His wisdom
Is ancient, too, and immense. The star
Is steady, like Plato, over the mountain.

If there were no wind we might, we think, hear
The earth grind on its axis, or history
Drip in darkness like a leaking pipe in the cellar.

HURT HAWKS

I

The broken pillar of the wing jags from the clotted
  shoulder,
The wing trails like a banner in defeat,
No more to use the sky forever but live with famine
And pain a few days: cat nor coyote
Will shorten the week of waiting for death, there is
  game without talons.
He stands under the oak-bush and waits
The lame feet of salvation; at night he remembers
  freedom
And flies in a dream, the dawns ruin it.
He is strong and pain is worse to the strong, incapacity
  is worse.
The curs of the day come and torment him
At distance, no one but death the redeemer will humble
  that head,
The intrepid readiness, the terrible eyes.
The wild God of the world is sometimes merciful to those
That ask mercy, not often to the arrogant.
You do not know him, you communal people, or you
  have forgotten him;
Intemperate and savage, the hawk remembers him;
Beautiful and wild, the hawks, and men that are dying,
  remember him.

I'd sooner, except the penalties, kill a man than a hawk;
    but the great redtail
Had nothing left but unable misery
From the bone too shattered for mending, the wing
    that trailed under his talons when he moved.
We had fed him six weeks, I gave him freedom,
He wandered over the foreland hill and returned in the
    evening, asking for death,
Not like a beggar, still eyed with the old
Implacable arrogance. I gave him the lead gift in the
    twilight. What fell was relaxed,
Owl-downy, soft feminine feathers; but what
Soared: the fierce rush: the night-herons by the flooded
    river cried fear at its rising
Before it was quite unsheathed from reality.

HAWK

This morning
　the hawk
　　rose up
　　　out of the meadow's browse

and swung over the lake –
　it settled
　　on the small black dome
　　　of a dead pine,

alert as an admiral,
　its profile
　　distinguished with sideburns
　　　the color of smoke,

and I said: remember
　this is not something
　　of the red fire, this is
　　　heaven's fistful

of death and destruction,
　and the hawk hooked
　　one exquisite foot
　　　onto a last twig

to look deeper
   into the yellow reeds
      along the edges of the water
         and I said: remember

the tree, the cave,
   the white lily of resurrection,
      and that's when it simply lifted
         its golden feet and floated

into the wind, belly-first,
   and then it cruised along the lake –
      all the time its eyes fastened
         harder than love on some

unimportant rustling in the
   yellow reeds – and then it
      seemed to crouch high in the air, and then it
         turned into a white blade, which fell.

THE SWAN

THE SILVER SWAN

The silver swan, who living had no note,
When death approached, unlocked her silent throat,
Leaning her breast against the reedy shore,
Thus sung her first and last, and sung no more:
Farewell all joys! O death, come close mine eyes;
More geese than swans now live, more fools than wise.

TWO SWANS
from Prothalamion

With that I saw two Swans of goodly hew
Come softly swimming down along the lee;
Two fairer Birds I yet did never see;
The snow, which doth the top of Pindus strew,
Did never whiter shew;
Nor Jove himself, when he a Swan would be,
For love of Leda, whiter did appear;
Yet Leda was (they say) as white as he,
Yet not so white as these, nor nothing near;
So purely white they were,
That even the gentle stream, the which them bare,
Seemed foul to them, and bade his billows spare
To wet their silken feathers, lest they might
Soil their fair plumes with water not so fair,
And mar their beauties bright,
That shone as heaven's light,
Against their Bridal day, which was not long:
    Sweet Thames! run softly, till I end my song.

THE DYING SWAN

The plain was grassy, wild and bare,
Wide, wild, and open to the air,
Which had built up everywhere
An under-roof of doleful grey.
With an inner voice the river ran,
Adown it floated a dying swan,
And loudly did it lament.
It was the middle of the day.
Even the weary wind went on,
And took the reed-tops as it went.

Some blue peaks in the distance rose,
And white against the cold-white sky,
Shone out their crowning snows.
One willow over the river wept,
And shook the wave as the wind did sigh;
Above in the wind was the swallow,
Chasing itself at its own wild will,
And far thro' the marish green and still
The tangled water-courses slept,
Shot over with purple, and green, and yellow.

The wild swan's death-hymn took the soul
Of that waste place with joy
Hidden in sorrow: at first to the ear

The warble was low, and full and clear;
And floating about the under-sky,
Prevailing in weakness, the coronach stole
Sometimes afar, and sometimes anear;
But anon her awful jubilant voice,
With a music strange and manifold,
Flow'd forth on a carol free and bold;

As when a mighty people rejoice
With shawms and cymbals, and harps of gold,
And the tumult of their acclaim is roll'd
Thro' the open gates of the city afar,
To the shepherd who watcheth the evening star.
And the creeping mosses and clambering weeds,
And the willow-branches hoar and dank,
And the wavy swell of the soughing reeds,
And the wave-worn horns of the echoing bank,
And the silvery marish-flowers that throng
The desolate creeks and pools among,
Were flooded over with eddying song.

THE SWAN

This laboring through what is still undone,
as though, legs bound, we hobbled along the way,
is like the awkward walking of the swan.

And dying – to let go, no longer feel
the solid ground we stand on every day –
is like his anxious letting himself fall

into the water, which receives him gently
and which, as though with reverence and joy,
draws back past him in streams on either side;
while, infinitely silent and aware,
in his full majesty and ever more
indifferent, he condescends to glide.

RAINER MARIA RILKE   151
TRANSLATED BY STEPHEN MITCHELL

WINTER SWAN

It is a hollow garden, under the cloud;
Beneath the heel a hollow earth is turned;
Within the mind the live blood shouts aloud;
Under the breast the willing blood is burned,
Shut with the fire passed and the fire returned.
But speak, you proud!
Where lies the leaf-caught world once thought
    abiding,
Now but a dry disarray and artifice?
Here, to the ripple cut by the cold, drifts this
Bird, the long throat bent back, and the eyes in hiding.

THE WILD SWANS AT COOLE

The trees are in their autumn beauty,
The woodland paths are dry,
Under the October twilight the water
Mirrors a still sky;
Upon the brimming water among the stones
Are nine-and-fifty swans.

The nineteenth autumn has come upon me
Since I first made my count;
I saw, before I had well finished,
All suddenly mount
And scatter wheeling in great broken rings
Upon their clamorous wings.

I have looked upon those brilliant creatures,
And now my heart is sore.
All's changed since I, hearing at twilight,
The first time on this shore,
The bell-beat of their wings above my head,
Trod with a lighter tread.

Unwearied still, lover by lover,
They paddle in the cold
Companionable streams or climb the air;
Their hearts have not grown old;

Passion or conquest, wander where they will,
Attend upon them still.

But now they drift on the still water,
Mysterious, beautiful;
Among what rushes will they build,
By what lake's edge or pool
Delight men's eyes when I awake some day
To find they have flown away?

WILD SWANS

I looked in my heart while the wild swans went over.
And what did I see I had not seen before?
Only a question less or a question more;
Nothing to match the flight of wild birds flying.
Tiresome heart, forever living and dying,
House without air, I leave you and lock your door.
Wild swans, come over the town, come over
The town again, trailing your legs and crying!

EDNA ST. VINCENT MILLAY

NESTS AND
CAGES

BIRDS' NESTS

How fresh the air, the birds how busy now!
In every walk if I but peep I find
Nests newly made or finished all and lined
With hair and thistledown, and in the bough
Of little hawthorn, huddled up in green,
The leaves still thickening as the spring gets age,
The pink's, quite round and snug and closely laid,
And linnet's of materials loose and rough;
And still hedge-sparrow, moping in the shade
Near the hedge-bottom, weaves of homely stuff,
Dead grass and mosses green, an hermitage,
For secrecy and shelter rightly made;
And beautiful it is to walk beside
The lanes and hedges where their homes abide.

BIRDS' NESTS

The summer nests uncovered by autumn wind,
Some torn, others dislodged, all dark,
Everyone sees them: low or high in tree,
Or hedge, or single bush, they hang like a mark.

Since there's no need of eyes to see them with
I cannot help a little shame
That I missed most, even at eye's level, till
The leaves blew off and made the seeing no game.

'Tis a light pang. I like to see the nests
Still in their places, now first known,
At home and by far roads. Boys never found them,
Whatever jays or squirrels may have done.

And most I like the winter nest deep hid
That leaves and berries fell into;
Once a dormouse dined there on hazel nuts;
And grass and goose-grass seeds found soil and grew.

A ROBIN'S NEST

Of the four fuchsia plants that hung
over the porch (the drooping
neck on every stem so heavy
with jeweled blooms they lost

all sense of posture), who's to say
what called one to a function other
than merely growing? Watering
the fourth one afternoon, I found

coiled within the elemental
circle of the plastic planter
a rustic imitation: the woven
ribbons of a robin's nest.

A perfect fit, like the band inside
the crown of a hat! And then the straw
of the nest itself became a hat –
a pillbox fortress, hardier

and taller all day long, because
of some law of nature whereby theft
is always rewarded. Ripping off
from trees these wisps of bark, as if

robbing Peter to pay Paul,
the bird would have the potted soil
as well – and so persuaded me
never to water it. I saw the eggs

a few days later, a four-eyed stare
of childish, uncomprehending blue –
lucky, like a four-leafed clover.
And then (but why the surprise?) the peep

of fluff above the top one morning,
like the stuffing of a padded
envelope torn open, and though
I read the message at a respectful

distance, even the fuzzy print
was easy to decipher. While
the vines were nearly dead, four buds
(less like the fuchsia's than a snap-

dragon's that never snapped) flung back
their heads on funny rubber necks,
beaks open in a parody
of ecstasy. And through the air

she swooped to them who couldn't see
what they'd been longing for – the tender
worm that streamed like a banner from
her beak, the lifted battle flag

of life's own bloody victory.

THE CAGE
from "The Manciple's Tale"

Tak any brid, and put it in a cage,
And do al thyn entente, and thy corage
To fostre it tendrely with mete and drinke,
Of alle deyntees that thou canst bithinke,
And kepe it al so clenly as thou may;
Al-though his cage of gold be never so gay,
Yet hath this brid, by twenty thousand fold,
Lever in a forest, that is rude and cold,
Gon ete wormes and swich wretchednesse.
For ever this brid wol doon his bisinesse
To escape out of his cage, if he may:
His liberty this brid desireth ay.

THREE THINGS TO REMEMBER

A robin redbreast in a cage
Puts all Heaven in a rage.

A skylark wounded on the wing
Doth make a cherub cease to sing.

He who shall hurt the little wren
Shall never be beloved by men.

THE CAGED GOLDFINCH

Within a churchyard, on a recent grave,
    I saw a little cage
That jailed a goldfinch. All was silence save
    Its hops from stage to stage.

There was inquiry in its wistful eye,
    And once it tried to sing;
Of him or her who placed it there, and why,
    No one knew anything.

THE CAGED SKYLARK

As a dare-gale skylark scanted in a dull cage
   Man's mounting spirit in his bone-house, mean
      house, dwells –
   That bird beyond the remembering his free fells,
This in drudgery, day-labouring-out life's age.

Though aloft on turf or perch or poor low stage,
   Both sing sometímes the sweetest, sweetest spells,
   Yet both droop deadly sómetimes in their cells
Or wring their barriers in bursts of fear or rage.

Not that the sweet-fowl, song-fowl, needs no rest –
Why, hear him, hear him babble and drop down
     to his nest,
   But his own nest, wild nest, no prison.

Man's spirit will be flesh-bound when found at best,
But uncumberèd: meadow-down is not distressed
   For a rainbow footing it nor he for his bónes rísen.

MARCHÉ AUX OISEAUX

Hundreds of birds are singing in the square.
Their minor voices fountaining in air
And constant as a fountain, lightly loud,
Do not drown out the burden of the crowd.

Far from his gold Sudan, the travailleur
Lends to the noise an intermittent chirr
Which to his hearers seems more joy than rage.
He batters softly at his wooden cage.

Here are the silver-bill, the orange-cheek,
The perroquet, the dainty coral-beak
Stacked in their cages; and around them move
The buyers in their termless hunt for love.

Here are the old, the ill, the imperial child;
The lonely people, desperate and mild;
The ugly; past these faces one can read
The tyranny of one outrageous need.

We love the small, said Burke. And if the small
Be not yet small enough, why then by Hell
We'll cramp it till it knows but how to feed,
And we'll provide the water and the seed.

FLY

I have been cruel to a fat pigeon
Because he would not fly
All he wanted was to live like a friendly old man

He had let himself become a wreck filthy and confiding
Wild for his food beating the cat off the garbage
Ignoring his mate perpetually snotty at the beak
Smelling waddling having to be
Carried up the ladder at night content

Fly I said throwing him into the air
But he would drop and run back expecting to be fed
I said it again and again throwing him up
As he got worse
He let himself be picked up every time
Until I found him in the dovecote dead
Of the needless efforts

So that is what I am

Pondering his eye that could not
Conceive that I was a creature to run from

I who have always believed too much in words

W. S. MERWIN   169

BIRDSONG

NEVER AGAIN WOULD BIRDS' SONG
BE THE SAME

He would declare and could himself believe
That the birds there in all the garden round
From having heard the daylong voice of Eve
Had added to their own an oversound,
Her tone of meaning but without the words.
Admittedly an eloquence so soft
Could only have had an influence on birds
When call or laughter carried it aloft.
Be that as may be, she was in their song.
Moreover her voice upon their voices crossed
Had now persisted in the woods so long
That probably it never would be lost.
Never again would birds' song be the same.
And to do that to birds was why she came.

BIRD-LANGUAGE

Trying to understand the words
    Uttered on all sides by birds,
I recognize in what I hear
    Noises that betoken fear.

Though some of them, I'm certain, must
    Stand for rage, bravado, lust,
All other notes that birds employ
    Sound like synonyms for joy.

THE SADDEST NOISE

The saddest noise, the sweetest noise,
   The maddest noise that grows, –
The birds, they make it in the spring,
   At night's delicious close.

Between the March and April line –
   That magical frontier
Beyond which summer hesitates,
   Almost too heavenly near.

It makes us think of all the dead
   That sauntered with us here,
By separation's sorcery
   Made cruelly more dear.

It makes us think of what we had,
   And what we now deplore.
We almost wish those siren throats
   Would go and sing no more.

An ear can break a human heart
   As quickly as a spear,
We wish the ear had not a heart
   So dangerously near.

EMILY DICKINSON

THE DOVE

How often, these hours, have I heard the monotonous
   crool of a dove –
Voice, low, insistent, obscure, since its nest it has hid
   in a grove –
Flowers of the linden wherethrough the hosts of the
   honey-bees rove.

And I have been busily idle: no problems; nothing
   to prove;
No urgent foreboding; but only life's shallow habitual
   groove:
Then why, if I pause to listen, should the languageless
   note of a dove
So dark with disquietude seem? And what is it
   sorrowing of?

A MINOR BIRD

I have wished a bird would fly away,
And not sing by my house all day;

Have clapped my hands at him from the door
When it seemed as if I could bear no more.

The fault must partly have been in me.
The bird was not to blame for his key.

And of course there must be something wrong
In wanting to silence any song.

FLIGHTS OF
FANCY

THE DEATH AND BURIAL
OF COCK ROBBIN

Here lies Cock Robbin dead and cold:
His end this book will soon unfold!

"Who did kill Cock Robbin?"
"I" said the sparrow, "with my bow and arrow,
I did kill Cock Robbin."

"Who did see him die?"
"I" said the fly, "with my little eye,
And I did see him die."

"And who catch'd his blood?"
"I" said the fish, "with my little dish,
And I catch'd his blood."

"And who did make his shroud?"
"I" said the beetle, "with my little needle,
And I did make his shroud."

"Who'll dig his grave?"
"I" said the owl,
"With my spade and show'l,
And I'll dig his grave."

"Who'll be the parson?"
"I" said the rook,
"With my little book,
And I'll be the parson."

"Who'll be the clerk?"
"I" said the lark,
"If 'tis not in the dark,
And I'll be the clerk."

"Who'll carry him to the grave?"
"I" said the kite,
"If 'tis not in the night,
And I'll carry him to the grave."

"Who'll carry the link?"
"I" said the linnet,
"I'll fetch it in a minute,
And I'll carry the link."

"Who'll be chief mourner?"
"I" said the swan,
"I'm sorry he's gone,
And I'll be chief mourner."

"Who'll bear the pall?"
"We" said the wren,

Both the cock and the hen,
"And we'll bear the pall."

"Who'll run before?"
"I" said the deer,
"I run fast for fear,
And I'll run before."

"Who'll sing a psalm?"
"I" said the thrush,
As she sat in a bush,
"And I'll sing a psalm."

"Who'll throw in the dirt?"
"I" said the fox,
"Though I steal hens and cocks,
I'll throw in the dirt."

"And who'll toll the bell?"
"I" said the bull,
"Because I can pull,
And so, Cock Robbin, farewell!"

All the birds of the air
Fell to sighing and sobbing,
When they heard the bell toll
For poor Cock Robbin.

ANON.

RONDEL

from The Parliament of Fowls

And whan this werk al brought was to an ende,
To every foul Nature yaf his make
By evene acord, and on here way they wende.
And, Lord, the blisse and joye that they make!
For ech of hem gan other in wynges take,
And with here nekkes ech gan other wynde,
Thankynge alwey the noble goddesse of kynde.

But fyrst were chosen foules for to synge,
As yer by yer was alwey hir usaunce
To synge a roundel at here departynge,
To don to Nature honour and plesaunce.
The note, I trowe, imaked was in Fraunce,
The wordes were swiche as ye may heer fynde,
The next vers, as I now have in mynde.

"Now welcome, somer, with thy sonne softe.
That hast this wintres wedres overshake,
And driven away the longe nyghtes blake!

"Saynt Valentyn, that art ful hy on-lofte,
Thus syngen smale foules for thy sake:
Now welcome, somer, with thy sonne softe,
That hast this wintres wedres overshake.

"Wel han they cause for to gladen ofte,
Sith ech of hem recovered hath hys make,
Ful blissful mowe they synge when they wake:
Now welcome, somer, with thy sonne softe,
That hast this wintres wedres overshake,
And driven away the longe nyghtes blake!"

MAGPIES

One, Sorrow,
Two, Mirth,
Three, a Wedding,
Four, a Birth,
Five, for Silver,
Six, for Gold,
Seven, for a secret not to be told,
Eight, for Heaven,
Nine, for Hell,
And Ten, for the devil's ain sel.

LITTLE BIRDS ARE PLAYING

Little Birds are playing
    Bagpipes on the shore,
    Where the tourists snore:
"Thanks!" they cry. "'Tis thrilling!
Take, oh, take, this shilling!
    Let us have no more!"

Little Birds are bathing
    Crocodiles in cream,
    Like a happy dream:
Like, but not so lasting –
Crocodiles, when fasting,
    Are not all they seem!

Little Birds are choking
    Baronets with bun,
    Taught to fire a gun:
Taught, I say, to splinter
Salmon in the winter –
    Merely for the fun.

Little Birds are hiding
    Crimes in carpet-bags,
    Blessed by happy stags:
Blessed, I say, though beaten –

Since our friends are eaten
    When the memory flags.

Little Birds are tasting
    Gratitude and gold,
    Pale with sudden cold;
Pale, I say, and wrinkled –
When the bells have tinkled,
    And the Tale is told.

THE OWL AND THE PUSSY-CAT

The Owl and the Pussy-Cat went to sea
     In a beautiful pea-green boat:
      They took some honey, and plenty of money
    Wrapped up in a five-pound note.
The Owl looked up to the stars above,
    And sang to a small guitar,
"Oh, lovely Pussy, oh, Pussy, my love,
    What a beautiful Pussy you are,
        You are,
        You are,
    What a beautiful Pussy you are!"

Pussy said to the Owl, "You elegant fowl,
    How charmingly sweet you sing!
Oh, let us be married; too long we have tarried:
    But what shall we do for a ring?"
They sailed away for a year and a day,
    To the land where the bong-tree grows;
And there in the wood a Piggy-wig stood,
    With a ring at the end of his nose,
        His nose,
        His nose,
    With a ring at the end of his nose.

"Dear Pig, are you willing to sell for one shilling
    Your ring?" Said the Piggy, "I will."
So they took it away and were married next day
    By the Turkey who lives on the hill.
They dined on mince and slices of quince,
    Which they ate with a runcible spoon;
And hand in hand, on the edge of the sand,
    They danced by the light of the moon,
            The moon,
            The moon,
    They danced by the light of the moon.

THE SEA-GULL

Hark to the whimper of the sea-gull;
He weeps because he's not an ea-gull.
Suppose you were, you silly sea-gull,
Could you explain it to your she-gull?

OGDEN NASH   191

THE PENGUIN JANE AUSTEN

With a single indecorous groan
a glacier calves an iceberg the size
of a cathedral into the christening sea.
Along the icefoot, ritual courtship

flurries the frigid air into squawks
and plumage, the shuffled chase
that observers, stomping their feet for warmth,
call dance. And after?

After a belle's dance card filled twice over
and a wallflower wilted with watching
territory staked step by measured step,
and the pecking order of kisses?

After the final bow,
after swallow-tailed males swooped
over the shimmer, the shiver
of jewel- and sweat-scaled females?

Up from the bed of lost feathers,
the mating for life. Under a sky
literate with *M's*, littered
with scavengers' winged *W's*,

two months stand still on the ice for him,
egg cradled on his melting feet.
For her the miles to retreating sea
to feed, then the longer walk back.

O cotillions and calling cards,
clergy waddling in wedding vestments,
marriage of property to title, awaiting issue,
how roughly do you compare?

A LISTENER'S GUIDE TO THE BIRDS

Wouldst know the lark?
Then hark!
Each natural bird
Must be seen *and* heard.
The lark's "Tee-ee" is a tinkling entreaty,
But it's not always "Tee-ee" –
Sometimes it's "Tee-titi."
    So watch yourself.

Birds have their love-and-mating song,
Their warning cry, their hating song;
Some have a night song, some a day song,
A lilt, a tilt, a come-what-may song;
Birds have their careless bough and teeter song
And, of course, their Roger Tory Peter song.

The studious ovenbird (pale pinkish legs)
Calls, "Teacher, teacher, teacher!"
The chestnut-sided warbler begs
To see Miss Beecher.
    "I wish to see Miss Beecher."
(Sometimes interpreted as "Please please please ta
    meetcha.")

The redwing (frequents swamps and marshes)
Gurgles, "Konk-la-reeee,"
Eliciting from the wood duck
The exclamation "Jeeee!"
    (But that's the *male* wood duck, remember.
    If it's his wife you seek,
    Wait till you hear a distressed "Whoo-eek!")

Nothing is simpler than telling a barn owl from a veery:
One says, "Kschh!" in a voice that is eerie,
The other says, "Vee-ur," in a manner that is breezy.
    (I told you it was easy.)
On the other hand, distinguishing between the veery
And the olive-backed thrush
Is another matter. It couldn't be worse.
The thrush's song is similar to the veery's,
Only it's in reverse.

Let us suppose you hear a bird say, "Fitz-bew,"
The things you can be sure of are two:
First, the bird is an alder flycatcher (*Empidonax traillii
    traillii*);
Second, you are standing in Ohio – or, as some people
    call it, O-hee-o –
Because, although it may come as a surprise to you,

The alder flycatcher, in New York or New England,
    does not say, "Fitz-bew,"
It says, "Wee-bé-o."

"Chu-chu-chu" is the note of the harrier,
Copied, of course, from our common carrier.
The osprey, thanks to a lucky fluke,
Avoids "Chu-chu" and cries, "Chewk, chewk!"
    So there's no difficulty there.

The chickadee likes to pronounce his name;
It's extremely helpful and adds to his fame.
But in spring you can get the heebie-jeebies
Untangling chickadees from phoebes.
The chickadee, when he's all afire,
Whistles, "Fee-bee," to express desire.
He should be arrested and thrown in jail
For impersonating another male.
    (There's a way you can tell which bird is which,
    But just the same, it's a nasty switch.)
Our gay deceiver may fancy-free be
But he never does fool a female phoebe.

Oh, sweet the random sounds of birds!
The old-squaw, practicing his thirds;
The distant bittern, driving stakes,
The lonely loon on haunted lakes;

The white-throat's pure and tenuous thread –
They go to my heart, they go to my head.
How hard it is to find the words
With which to sing the praise of birds!
Yet birds, when *they* get singing praises,
Don't lack for words – they know some daisies:
  "Fitz-bew,"
  "Konk-la-reeee,"
  "Hip-three-cheers,"
  "Onk-a-lik, ow-owdle-ow,"
  "Cheedle cheedle chew,"
And dozens of other inspired phrases.

E. B. WHITE   197

THE BIRD

The Bird, most ardent for life of all our blood kin,
lives out a singular destiny on the frontier of day. As a
migrant whom the sun's inflation haunts, he journeys
by night because the days are too short for him. In
times of grey moon, grey as mistletoe of the Gauls, he
peoples with his ghost the prophecy of the nights.
And his cry in the night is a cry of dawn itself: a cry of
holy war and naked steel.

On the cross-beam of his wing is the vast balancing
of a double season, and under the curve of his flight
the very curvature of the earth. Alternation is his law,
ambiguity his reign. In the space and time that he
broods over in one flight, a single summering is
heresy. It is likewise the scandal of painter and poet,
who bring seasons together at that height where all
intersect.

Austerity of flight! . . . Most avid for existence of all
who share our table, the bird is he who bears hidden
in himself, to nourish his passion, the highest fever of
the blood. His grace is in that burning. Nothing
symbolic about this: it is a simple biological fact. And
so light in our view is the stuff of birds, that against
the fire of day it seems to reach incandescence. A man

at sea, feeling noon in the air, lifts his head at this
wonder: a white gull opened on the sky, like a
woman's hand before the flame of a lamp, elevating in
daylight the pink translucence of a host, a wafer's
whiteness . . .

Sickle-shaped wing of dream, you will find us again
this evening on other shores!

LEGENDARY
AND
EMBLEMATIC
BIRDS

THE HARPIES
from the Aeneid, Book III

At length I land upon the Strophades,
Safe from the danger of the stormy seas.
Those isles are compass'd by th' Ionian main,
The dire abode where the foul Harpies reign,
Forc'd by the winged warriors to repair
To their old homes, and leave their costly fare.
Monsters more fierce offended Heav'n ne'er sent
From hell's abyss, for human punishment:
With virgin faces, but with wombs obscene,
Foul paunches, and with ordure still unclean;
With claws for hands, and looks for ever lean.

    "We landed at the port, and soon beheld
Fat herds of oxen graze the flow'ry field,
And wanton goats without a keeper stray'd.
With weapons we the welcome prey invade,
Then call the gods for partners of our feast,
And Jove himself, the chief invited guest.
We spread the tables on the greensward ground;
We feed with hunger, and the bowls go round;
When from the mountain-tops, with hideous cry,
And clatt'ring wings, the hungry Harpies fly;
They snatch the meat, defiling all they find,
And, parting, leave a loathsome stench behind.
Close by a hollow rock, again we sit,

New dress the dinner, and the beds refit,
Secure from sight, beneath a pleasing shade,
Where tufted trees a native arbor made.
Again the holy fires on altars burn;
And once again the rav'nous birds return,
Or from the dark recesses where they lie,
Or from another quarter of the sky;
With filthy claws their odious meal repeat,
And mix their loathsome ordures with their meat.
I bid my friends for vengeance then prepare,
And with the hellish nation wage the war.
They, as commanded, for the fight provide,
And in the grass their glitt'ring weapons hide;
Then, when along the crooked shore we hear
Their clatt'ring wings, and saw the foes appear,
Misenus sounds a charge: we take th' alarm,
And our strong hands with swords and bucklers arm.
In this new kind of combat all employ
Their utmost force, the monsters to destroy.
In vain – the fated skin is proof to wounds;
And from their plumes the shining sword rebounds.
At length rebuff'd, they leave their mangled prey,
And their stretch'd pinions to the skies display.

TRANSLATED BY JOHN DRYDEN

HUNDRED-SUNNED PHENIX

O blest unfabled Incense Tree
That burns in glorious Araby,
With red scent chalicing the air
Till earth-life grow Elysian there!

Half buried to her flaming breast
In this bright tree, she makes her nest,
Hundred-sunned Phenix! when she must
Crumble at length to hoary dust!

Her gorgeous death-bed! her rich pyre
Burnt up with aromatic fire!
Her urn, sight high from spoiler men!
Her birthplace when self-born again!

The mountainless green wilds among
Here ends she her unechoing song!
With amber tears and odorous sighs
Mourned by the desert where she dies!

LEDA AND THE SWAN

A sudden blow: the great wings beating still
Above the staggering girl, her thighs caressed
By the dark webs, her nape caught in his bill,
He holds her helpless breast upon his breast.

How can those terrified vague fingers push
The feathered glory from her loosening thighs?
And how can body, laid in that white rush,
But feel the strange heart beating where it lies?

A shudder in the loins engenders there
The broken wall, the burning roof and tower
And Agamemnon dead.
                   Being so caught up,
So mastered by the brute blood of the air,
Did she put on his knowledge with his power
Before the indifferent beak could let her drop?

THE LIVING QUETZALCOATL

I am the Living Quetzalcoatl.
Naked I come from out of the deep
From the place which I call my Father,
Naked have I travelled the long way round
From heaven, past the sleeping sons of God.

Out of the depths of the sky, I came like an eagle.
Out of the bowels of the earth like a snake.

All things that lift in the lift of living between earth
        and sky, know me.

But I am the inward star invisible.
And the star is the lamp in the hand of the
        Unknown Mover.
Beyond me is a Lord who is terrible, and wonderful,
        and dark to me forever.
Yet I have lain in his loins, ere he begot me in
        Mother space.

Now I am alone on earth and this is mine.
The roots are mine, down the dark, moist path of the snake.
And the branches are mine, in the paths of the sky
        and the bird,
But the spark of me that is me is more than mine own.

And the feet of men, and the hands of the women
    know me.
And knees and thighs and loins, and the bowels of
    strength and seed are lit with me.
The snake of my left-hand out of the darkness is
    kissing your feet with his mouth of caressive fire,
And putting his strength in your heels and ankles, his
    flame in your knees and your legs and your loins,
    his circle of rest in your belly.
For I am Quetzalcoatl, the feathered snake.
And I am not with you till my serpent has coiled his
    circle of rest in your belly.
And I, Quetzalcoatl, the eagle of the air, am brushing
    your faces with vision.
I am fanning your breasts with my breath.
And building my nest of peace in your bones.
I am Quetzalcoatl, of the Two Ways.

PERSUASION
after Bede

"Man's life is like a Sparrow, mighty King!
That – while at banquet with your Chiefs you sit
Housed near a blazing fire – is seen to flit
Safe from the wintry tempest. Fluttering,
Here did it enter; there, on hasty wing,
Flies out, and passes on from cold to cold;
But whence it came we know not, nor behold
Whither it goes. Even such, that transient Thing,
The human Soul; not utterly unknown
While in the Body lodged, her warm abode;
But from what world She came, what woe or weal
On her departure waits, no tongue hath shown;
This mystery if the Stranger can reveal,
His be a welcome cordially bestowed!"

WILLIAM WORDSWORTH

From THE RIME OF THE ANCIENT MARINER

"And now the Storm-blast came, and he
Was tyrannous and strong;
He struck with his o'ertaking wings,
And chased us south along.

With sloping masts and dipping prow,
As who pursued with yell and blow
Still treads the shadow of his foe,
And forward bends his head,
The ship drove fast, loud roared the blast,
And southward aye we fled.

And now there came both mist and snow,
And it grew wondrous cold:
And ice, mast-high, came floating by,
As green as emerald.

And through the drifts the snowy clifts
Did send a dismal sheen:
Nor shapes of men nor beasts we ken –
The ice was all between.

The ice was here, the ice was there,
The ice was all around:

It cracked and growled, and roared and howled,
Like noises in a swound!

At length did cross an Albatross,
Thorough the fog it came;
As if it had been a Christian soul,
We hailed it in God's name.

It ate the food it ne'er had eat,
And round and round it flew.
The ice did split with a thunder-fit;
The helmsman steered us through!

And a good south wind sprung up behind;
The Albatross did follow,
And every day, for food or play,
Came to the mariners' hollo!

In mist or cloud, on mast or shroud,
It perched for vespers nine;
Whiles all the night, through fog-smoke white,
Glimmered the white Moon-shine."

"God save thee, ancient Mariner!
From the fiends, that plague thee thus! –
Why look'st thou so?" – With my crossbow
I shot the ALBATROSS.

SAMUEL TAYLOR COLERIDGE

THE ALBATROSS

Often, for pastime, mariners will ensnare
The albatross, that vast sea-bird who sweeps
On high companionable pinion where
Their vessel glides upon the bitter deeps.

Torn from his native space, this captive king
Flounders upon the deck in stricken pride,
And pitiably lets his great white wing
Drag like a heavy paddle at his side.

This rider of winds, how awkward he is, and weak!
How droll he seems, who was all grace of late!
A sailor pokes a pipestem into his beak,
Another, hobbling, mocks his trammeled gait.

The Poet is like this monarch of the clouds,
Familiar of storms, of stars, and of all high things;
Exiled on earth amidst its hooting crowds,
He cannot walk, borne down by giant wings.

212   CHARLES BAUDELAIRE
      TRANSLATED BY RICHARD WILBUR

TO A SKYLARK

Hail to thee, blithe Spirit!
    Bird thou never wert,
  That from Heaven, or near it,
    Pourest thy full heart
In profuse strains of unpremeditated art.

  Higher still and higher
    From the earth thou springest
Like a cloud of fire;
    The blue deep thou wingest,
And singing still dost soar, and soaring ever singest.

In the golden lightning
    Of the sunken sun,
O'er which clouds are bright'ning,
    Thou dost float and run;
Like an unbodied joy whose race is just begun.

The pale purple even
    Melts around thy flight;
Like a star of Heaven,
    In the broad daylight
Thou art unseen, but yet I hear thy shrill delight,

Keen as are the arrows
    Of that silver sphere,

Whose intense lamp narrows
      In the white dawn clear
Until we hardly see – we feel that it is there.

All the earth and air
      With thy voice is loud,
As, when night is bare,
      From one lonely cloud
The moon rains out her beams, and Heaven is overflowed.

What thou art we know not;
      What is most like thee?
From rainbow clouds there flow not
      Drops so bright to see
As from thy presence showers a rain of melody.

Like a Poet hidden
      In the light of thought,
Singing hymns unbidden,
      Till the world is wrought
To sympathy with hopes and fears it heeded not:

Like a high-born maiden
      In a palace-tower,
Soothing her love-laden
      Soul in secret hour
With music sweet as love, which overflows her bower:

Like a glow-worm golden
    In a dell of dew,
Scattering unbeholden
    Its aëreal hue
Among the flowers and grass, which screen it from
    the view!

Like a rose embowered
    In its own green leaves,
By warm winds deflowered,
    Till the scent it gives
Makes faint with too much sweet those heavy-wingèd
    thieves:

Sound of vernal showers
    On the twinkling grass,
Rain-awakened flowers,
    All that ever was
Joyous, and clear, and fresh, thy music doth surpass:

Teach us, Sprite or Bird,
    What sweet thoughts are thine:
I have never heard
    Praise of love or wine
That panted forth a flood of rapture so divine.

Chorus Hymeneal,
    Or triumphal chant,

Matched with thine would be all
    But an empty vaunt,
A thing wherein we feel there is some hidden want.

    What objects are the fountains
        Of thy happy strain?
    What fields, or waves, or mountains?
        What shapes of sky or plain?
What love of thine own kind? what ignorance of pain?

    With thy clear keen joyance
        Languor cannot be:
    Shadow of annoyance
        Never came near thee:
Thou lovest – but ne'er knew love's sad satiety.

    Waking or asleep,
        Thou of death must deem
    Things more true and deep
        Than we mortals dream,
Or how could thy notes flow in such a crystal stream?

    We look before and after,
        And pine for what is not:
    Our sincerest laughter
        With some pain is fraught;
Our sweetest songs are those that tell of saddest thought.

Yet if we could scorn
    Hate, and pride, and fear;
If we were things born
    Not to shed a tear,
I know not how thy joy we ever should come near.

Better than all measures
    Of delightful sound,
Better than all treasures
    That in books are found,
Thy skill to poet were, thou scorner of the ground!

Teach me half the gladness
    That thy brain must know,
Such harmonious madness
    From my lips would flow
The world should listen then – as I am listening now.

PERCY BYSSHE SHELLEY   217

ODE TO A NIGHTINGALE

My heart aches, and a drowsy numbness pains
   My sense, as though of hemlock I had drunk,
Or emptied some dull opiate to the drains
   One minute past, and Lethe-wards had sunk:
'Tis not through envy of thy happy lot
   But being too happy in thine happiness, –
      That thou, light-winged Dryad of the trees,
        In some melodious plot
   Of beechen green, and shadows numberless,
     Singest of summer in full-throated ease.

O, for a draught of vintage! that hath been
   Cool'd a long age in the deep-delved earth,
Tasting of Flora and the country green,
   Dance, and Provençal song, and sunburnt mirth!
O for a beaker full of the warm South,
   Full of the true, the blushful Hippocrene,
      With beaded bubbles winking at the brim,
        And purple-stained mouth;
   That I might drink, and leave the world unseen,
     And with thee fade away into the forest dim:

Fade far away, dissolve, and quite forget
   What thou among the leaves hast never known,
The weariness, the fever, and the fret

Here, where men sit and hear each other groan;
Where palsy shakes a few, sad, last gray hairs,
    Where youth grows pale, and spectre-thin, and dies;
        Where but to think is to be full of sorrow
            And leaden-eyed despairs,
    Where Beauty cannot keep her lustrous eyes,
        Or new Love pine at them beyond to-morrow.

Away! away! for I will fly to thee,
    Not charioted by Bacchus and his pards,
But on the viewless wings of Poesy,
    Though the dull brain perplexes and retards:
Already with thee! tender is the night,
    And haply the Queen-Moon is on her throne,
        Cluster'd around by all her starry Fays;
                But here there is no light,
    Save what from heaven is with the breezes blown
        Through verdurous glooms and winding mossy
            ways.

I cannot see what flowers are at my feet,
    Nor what soft incense hangs upon the boughs,
But, in embalmed darkness, guess each sweet
    Wherewith the seasonable month endows
The grass, the thicket, and the fruit-tree wild;
    White hawthorn, and the pastoral eglantine;
        Fast fading violets cover'd up in leaves;

And mid-May's eldest child,
The coming musk-rose, full of dewy wine,
    The murmurous haunt of flies on summer eves.

Darkling I listen; and, for many a time
    I have been half in love with easeful Death,
Call'd him soft names in many a mused rhyme,
    To take into the air my quiet breath;
Now more than ever seems it rich to die,
    To cease upon the midnight with no pain,
        While thou art pouring forth thy soul abroad
            In such an ecstasy!
    Still wouldst thou sing, and I have ears in vain –
        To thy high requiem become a sod.

Thou wast not born for death, immortal Bird!
    No hungry generations tread thee down;
The voice I hear this passing night was heard
    In ancient days by emperor and clown:
Perhaps the self-same song that found a path
    Through the sad heart of Ruth, when, sick for home,
        She stood in tears amid the alien corn;
            The same that oft-times hath
    Charm'd magic casements, opening on the foam
        Of perilous seas, in faery lands forlorn.

Forlorn! the very word is like a bell
   To toll me back from thee to my sole self!
Adieu! the fancy cannot cheat so well
   As she is fam'd to do, deceiving elf.
Adieu! adieu! thy plaintive anthem fades
   Past the near meadows, over the still stream,
      Up the hill-side; and now 'tis buried deep
         In the next valley-glades:
   Was it a vision, or a waking dream?
      Fled is that music: – Do I wake or sleep?

THE DARKLING THRUSH

I leant upon a coppice gate
    When Frost was spectre-gray,
And Winter's dregs made desolate
    The weakening eye of day.
The tangled bine-stems scored the sky
    Like strings of broken lyres,
And all mankind that haunted nigh
    Had sought their household fires.

The land's sharp features seemed to be
    The Century's corpse outleant,
His crypt the cloudy canopy,
    The wind his death-lament.
The ancient pulse of germ and birth
    Was shrunken hard and dry,
And every spirit upon earth
    Seemed fervourless as I.

At once a voice arose among
    The bleak twigs overhead
In a full-hearted evensong
    Of joy illimited;
An aged thrush, frail, gaunt, and small,
    In blast-beruffled plume,
Had chosen thus to fling his soul
    Upon the growing gloom.

So little cause for carolings
    Of such ecstatic sound
Was written on terrestrial things
    Afar or nigh around,
That I could think there trembled through
    His happy good-night air
Some blessed Hope, whereof he knew
    And I was unaware.

THOMAS HARDY

THE WINDHOVER
to Christ our Lord

I caught this morning morning's minion, king-
    dom of daylight's dauphin, dapple-dáwn-drawn
      Falcon, in his riding
    Of the rólling level úndernéath him steady áir,
      and stríding
High there, how he rung upon the rein of a
    wimpling wing,
In his ecstasy! then off, off forth on swing,
    As a skate's heel sweeps smooth on a bow-bend:
      the hurl and gliding
    Rebuffed the big wind. My heart in hiding
Stirred for a bird, – the achieve of, the mastery of the
    thing!

Brute beauty and valour and act, oh, air, pride,
    plume, here
    Buckle! AND the fire that breaks from thee then,
      a billion
Times told lovelier, more dangerous, O my chevalier!

    No wónder of it: shéer plód makes plóugh down síllion
Shine, and blue-bleak embers, ah my dear,
    Fall, gáll themsélves, and gásh góld-vermílion.

TO A WATERFOWL

Whither, midst falling dew,
While glow the heavens with the last steps of day,
Far, through their rosy depths, dost thou pursue
    Thy solitary way?

Vainly the fowler's eye
Might mark thy distant flight to do thee wrong,
As, darkly seen against the crimson sky,
    Thy figure floats along.

Seek'st thou the plashy brink
Of weedy lake, or marge of river wide,
Or where the rocking billows rise and sink
    On the chafed ocean-side?

There is a Power whose care
Teaches thy way along that pathless coast –
The desert and illimitable air –
    Lone wandering, but not lost.

All day thy wings have fanned,
At that far height, the cold, thin atmosphere,
Yet stoop not, weary, to the welcome land,
    Though the dark night is near.

And soon that toil shall end;
Soon shalt thou find a summer home, and rest,
And scream among thy fellows; reeds shall bend,
        Soon, o'er thy sheltered nest.

    Thou'rt gone, the abyss of heaven
Hath swallowed up thy form; yet, on my heart
Deeply has sunk the lesson thou hast given,
        And shall not soon depart.

    He who, from zone to zone,
Guides through the boundless sky thy certain flight,
In the long way that I must tread alone,
        Will lead my steps aright.

THE RAVEN

Once upon a midnight dreary, while I pondered,
    weak and weary,
Over many a quaint and curious volume of forgotten lore,
While I nodded, nearly napping, suddenly there came
    a tapping,
As of some one gently rapping, rapping at my
    chamber door.
"'Tis some visiter," I muttered, "tapping at my
    chamber door –
                Only this, and nothing more."

Ah, distinctly I remember it was in the bleak December,
And each separate dying ember wrought its ghost upon
    the floor.
Eagerly I wished the morrow; – vainly I had sought
    to borrow
From my books surcease of sorrow – sorrow for the
    lost Lenore –
For the rare and radiant maiden whom the angels
    name Lenore –
                Nameless here for evermore.

And the silken sad uncertain rustling of each purple
    curtain
Thrilled me – filled me with fantastic terrors never
    felt before;

So that now, to still the beating of my heart,
    I stood repeating
" 'Tis some visiter entreating entrance at my
    chamber door —
Some late visiter entreating entrance at my
    chamber door; —
            This it is, and nothing more."

Presently my soul grew stronger; hesitating then
    no longer,
"Sir," said I, "or Madam, truly your forgiveness I implore;
But the fact is I was napping, and so gently you
    came rapping,
And so faintly you came tapping, tapping at my
    chamber door,
That I scarce was sure I heard you" — here I opened
    wide the door; —
            Darkness there, and nothing more.

Deep into that darkness peering, long I stood there
    wondering, fearing,
Doubting, dreaming dreams no mortal ever dared
    to dream before;
But the silence was unbroken, and the darkness gave
    no token,
And the only word there spoken was the whispered
    word, "Lenore!"

This I whispered, and an echo murmured back the word,
    "Lenore!"
                Merely this and nothing more.

Back into the chamber turning, all my soul within
    me burning,
Soon again I heard a tapping somewhat louder
    than before.
"Surely," said I, "surely that is something at my
    window lattice;
Let me see, then, what thereat is, and this mystery
    explore –
Let my heart be still a moment and this mystery
    explore; –
                'Tis the wind and nothing more!"

Open here I flung the shutter, when, with many a
    flirt and flutter,
In there stepped a stately raven of the saintly days
    of yore.
Not the least obeisance made he; not an instant stopped
    or stayed he;
But, with mien of lord or lady, perched above my
    chamber door –
Perched upon a bust of Pallas just above my
    chamber door –
                Perched, and sat, and nothing more.

Then this ebony bird beguiling my sad fancy into
     smiling,
By the grave and stern decorum of the countenance
     it wore,
"Though thy crest be shorn and shaven, thou," I said,
     "art sure no craven,
Ghastly grim and ancient raven wandering from the
     Nightly shore –
Tell me what thy lordly name is on the Night's
     Plutonian shore!"
                    Quoth the raven, "Nevermore."

Much I marvelled this ungainly fowl to hear discourse
     so plainly,
Though its answer little meaning – little relevancy bore;
For we cannot help agreeing that no living human being
Ever yet was blessed with seeing bird above his chamber
     door –
Bird or beast upon the sculptured bust above his chamber
     door,
                    With such name as "Nevermore."

But the raven, sitting lonely on the placid bust, spoke only
That one word, as if his soul in that one word he did
     outpour.
Nothing further then he uttered – not a feather then
     he fluttered –

Till I scarcely more than muttered, "Other friends have
    flown before –
On the morrow *he* will leave me, as my hopes have flown
    before."
        Then the bird said, "Nevermore."

.   .   .   .   .   .

"Prophet!" said I, "thing of evil! – prophet still, if bird or
    devil! –
Whether Tempter sent, or whether tempest tossed
    thee here ashore,
Desolate yet all undaunted, on this desert land
    enchanted –
On this home by Horror haunted – tell me truly,
    I implore –
Is there – *is* there balm in Gilead? – tell me – tell me,
    I implore!"
        Quoth the raven, "Nevermore."

.   .   .   .   .   .

THIRTEEN WAYS OF LOOKING
AT A BLACKBIRD

I

Among twenty snowy mountains,
The only moving thing
Was the eye of the blackbird.

II

I was of three minds,
Like a tree
In which there are three blackbirds.

III

The blackbird whirled in the autumn winds.
It was a small part of the pantomime.

IV

A man and a woman
Are one.
A man and a woman and a blackbird
Are one.

V

I do not know which to prefer,
The beauty of inflections
Or the beauty of innuendoes,

The blackbird whistling
Or just after.

VI

Icicles filled the long window
With barbaric glass.
The shadow of the blackbird
Crossed it, to and fro.
The mood
Traced in the shadow
An indecipherable cause.

VII

O thin men of Haddam,
Why do you imagine golden birds?
Do you not see how the blackbird
Walks around the feet
Of the women about you?

VIII

I know noble acccents
And lucid, inescapable rhythms;
But I know, too,
That the blackbird is involved
In what I know.

IX

When the blackbird flew out of sight,

It marked the edge
Of one of many circles.

X

At the sight of blackbirds
Flying in a green light,
Even the bawds of euphony
Would cry out sharply.

XI

He rode over Connecticut
In a glass coach.
Once, a fear pierced him,
In that he mistook
The shadow of his equipage
For blackbirds.

XII

The river is moving.
The blackbird must be flying.

XIII

It was evening all afternoon.
It was snowing
And it was going to snow.
The blackbird sat
In the cedar-limbs.

THE OVEN BIRD

There is a singer everyone has heard,
Loud, a mid-summer and a mid-wood bird,
Who makes the solid tree trunks sound again.
He says that leaves are old and that for flowers
Mid-summer is to spring as one to ten.
He says the early petal-fall is past
When pear and cherry bloom went down in showers
On sunny days a moment overcast;
And comes that other fall we name the fall.
He says the highway dust is over all.
The bird would cease and be as other birds
But that he knows in singing not to sing.
The question that he frames in all but words
Is what to make of a diminished thing.

OUT OF THE CRADLE ENDLESSLY
ROCKING

Out of the cradle endlessly rocking,
Out of the mocking-bird's throat, the musical shuttle,
Out of the Ninth-month midnight,
Over the sterile sands and the fields beyond, where the
      child leaving his bed wander'd alone, bareheaded,
      barefoot,
Down from the shower'd halo,
Up from the mystic play of shadows twining and
      twisting as if they were alive,
Out from the patches of briers and blackberries,
From the memories of the bird that chanted to me,
From your memories sad brother, from the fitful
      risings and fallings I heard,
From under that yellow half-moon late-risen and
      swollen as if with tears,
From those beginning notes of yearning and love there
      in the mist,
From the thousand responses of my heart never
      to cease,
From the myriad thence-arous'd words,
From the word stronger and more delicious than any,
From such as now they start the scene revisiting,
As a flock, twittering, rising, or overhead passing,
Borne hither, ere all eludes me, hurriedly,

A man, yet by these tears a little boy again,
Throwing myself on the sand, confronting the waves,
I, chanter of pains and joys, uniter of here and hereafter,
Taking all hints to use them, but swiftly leaping
    beyond them,
A reminiscence sing.

Once Paumanok,
When the lilac-scent was in the air and Fifth-month
    grass was growing,
Up this seashore in some briers,
Two feather'd guests from Alabama, two together,
And their nest, and four light-green eggs spotted with
    brown,
And every day the he-bird to and fro near at hand,
And every day the she-bird crouch'd on her nest, silent,
    with bright eyes,
And every day I, a curious boy, never too close, never
    disturbing them,
Cautiously peering, absorbing, translating.

Shine! shine! shine!
Pour down your warmth, great sun!
While we bask, we two together.

Two together!
Winds blow south, or winds blow north,

Day come white, or night come black,
Home, or rivers and mountains from home,
Singing all time, minding no time,
While we two keep together.

Till of a sudden,
May-be kill'd, unknown to her mate,
One forenoon the she-bird crouch'd not on the nest,
Nor return'd that afternoon, nor the next,
Nor ever appear'd again.

And thenceforward all summer in the sound of the sea,
And at night under the full of the moon in calmer
      weather,
Over the hoarse surging of the sea,
Or flitting from brier to brier by day,
I saw, I heard at intervals the remaining one, the he-bird,
The solitary guest from Alabama.

Blow! blow! blow!
Blow up sea-winds along Paumanok's shore;
I wait and I wait till you blow my mate to me.

Yes, when the stars glisten'd,
All night long on the prong of a moss-scallop'd stake,
Down almost amid the slapping waves,
Sat the lone singer wonderful causing tears.

He call'd on his mate,
He pour'd forth the meanings which I of all men know.

Yes my brother I know,
The rest might not, but I have treasur'd every note,
For more than once dimly down to the beach gliding,
Silent, avoiding the moonbeams, blending myself with
    the shadows,
Recalling now the obscure shapes, the echoes, the
    sounds and sights after their sorts,
The white arms out in the breakers tirelessly tossing,

I, with bare feet, a child, the wind wafting my hair,
Listen'd long and long.

Listen'd to keep, to sing, now translating the notes,
Following you my brother.

Soothe! soothe! soothe!
Close on its wave soothes the wave behind,
And again another behind embracing and lapping, every
    one close,
But my love soothes not me, not me.

Low hangs the moon, it rose late,
It is lagging— O I think it is heavy with love, with love.

O madly the sea pushes upon the land,
With love, with love.

O night! do I not see my love fluttering out among the
      breakers?
What is that little black thing I see there in the white?

Loud! loud! loud!
Loud I call to you, my love!

High and clear I shoot my voice over the waves,
Surely you must know who is here, is here,
You must know who I am, my love.

Low-hanging moon!
What is that dusky spot in your brown yellow?
O it is the shape, the shape of my mate!
O moon do not keep her from me any longer.

Land! land! O land!
Whichever way I turn, O I think you could give me my mate
      back again if you only would,
For I am almost sure I see her dimly whichever way I look.

O rising stars!
Perhaps the one I want so much will rise, will rise with some
      of you.

O throat! O trembling throat!
Sound clearer through the atmosphere!
Pierce the woods, the earth,
Somewhere listening to catch you must be the one I want.

. . . . . .

Hither my love!
Here I am! here!
With this just-sustain'd note I announce myself to you,
This gentle call is for you my love, for you.

Do not be decoy'd elsewhere,
That is the whistle of the wind, it is not my voice,
That is the fluttering, the fluttering of the spray,
Those are the shadows of leaves.

O darkness! O in vain!
O I am very sick and sorrowful.
O brown halo in the sky near the moon, drooping upon the sea!
O troubled reflection in the sea!
O throat! O throbbing heart!
And I singing uselessly, uselessly all the night.

O past! O happy life! O songs of joy!
In the air, in the woods, over fields,
Loved! loved! loved! loved! loved!
But my mate no more, no more with me!
We two altogether no more.

The aria sinking,
All else continuing, the stars shining,
The winds blowing, the notes of the bird continuous
    echoing,
With angry moans the fierce old mother incessantly
    moaning,
On the sands of Paumanok's shore gray and rustling,
The yellow half-moon enlarged, sagging down,
    drooping, the face of the sea almost touching,
The boy ecstatic, with his bare feet the waves, with his
    hair the atmosphere dallying,
The love in the heart long pent, now loose, now at last
    tumultuously bursting,
The aria's meaning, the ears, the soul, swiftly depositing,
The strange tears down the cheeks coursing,
The colloquy there, the trio, each uttering,
The undertone, the savage old mother incessantly
    crying,
To the boy's soul's questions sullenly timing, some
    drown'd secret hissing,
To the outsetting bard....

SAILING TO BYZANTIUM

I

That is no country for old men. The young
In one another's arms, birds in the trees,
– Those dying generations – at their song,
The salmon-falls, the mackerel-crowded seas,
Fish, flesh, or fowl, commend all summer long
Whatever is begotten, born, and dies.
Caught in that sensual music all neglect
Monuments of unageing intellect.

II

An aged man is but a paltry thing,
A tattered coat upon a stick, unless
Soul clap its hands and sing, and louder sing
For every tatter in its mortal dress,
Nor is there singing school but studying
Monuments of its own magnificence;
And therefore I have sailed the seas and come
To the holy city of Byzantium.

III

O sages standing in God's holy fire
As in the gold mosaic of a wall,
Come from the holy fire, perne in a gyre,
And be the singing-masters of my soul.

Consume my heart away; sick with desire
And fastened to a dying animal
It knows not what it is; and gather me
Into the artifice of eternity.

IV

Once out of nature I shall never take
My bodily form from any natural thing,
But such a form as Grecian goldsmiths make
Of hammered gold and gold enamelling
To keep a drowsy Emperor awake;
Or set upon a golden bough to sing
To lords and ladies of Byzantium
Of what is past, or passing, or to come.

ACKNOWLEDGMENTS

Thanks are due to the following copyright holders for their
permission to reprint:

ADCOCK, FLEUR: 'Love's Agent', from *The Virgin and the Nightingale,
Medieval Latin Poems*. Copyright © 1983 and reprinted by permission
of Bloodaxe Books. ATWOOD, MARGARET: 'Vultures', from *Poems
1976–1986* by Margaret Atwood. Copyright © 1987 by Margaret
Atwood. Reprinted by permission of Houghton Mifflin Company. All
rights reserved. Previously published in *True Stories* (1981). AUDEN,
W. H.: 'Bird-Language', from *W. H. Auden, Collected Poems* by W. H.
Auden, edited by Edward Mendelson. Copyright © 1969 by W. H.
Auden. Reprinted by permission of Random House, Inc. BAUDELAIRE,
CHARLES, tr. Richard Howard: 'Owls', from *Les Fleurs du Mal* by
Charles Baudelaire. Reprinted by permission of David R. Godine,
Publisher, Inc. Translation copyright © 1983 by Richard Howard.
BISHOP, ELIZABETH: 'Sandpiper', from *The Complete Poems 1927–1979*
by Elizabeth Bishop. Copyright © 1979, 1983 by Alice Helen
Methfessel. Reprinted by permission of Farrar, Straus and Giroux,
LLC. BOGAN, LOUISE: 'Winter Swan', from *The Blue Estuaries* by
Louise Bogan. Copyright © 1968 by Louise Bogan. Copyright
renewed 1996 by Ruth Limmer. BULLETT, GERALD: 'Woodpecker'
reprinted by permission of Everyman Publishers Plc. CLAMPITT,
AMY: 'A Whippoorwill in the Woods' and 'The Kingfisher', from
Collected Poems by Amy Clampitt. Copyright © 1997 by the Estate of
Amy Clampitt. Reprinted by permission of Alfred A. Knopf, a
division of Random House, Inc. DE LA MARE, WALTER: 'The Dove',
'Jenny Wren' and 'The Owl' by Walter de la Mare. Reprinted by
permission of The Literary Trustees of Walter de la Mare, and the
Society of Authors as their representative. DICKINSON, EMILY: 'The
Jay' and 'The Saddest Noise' by Emily Dickinson. Reprinted by
permission of the publishers and The Trustees of Amherst College
from *The Poems of Emily Dickinson*, Ralph W. Franklin, ed.,
Cambridge, Mass.: The Belknap Press of Harvard University Press,

245

247

248

INDEX OF AUTHORS

251